MUSIC LIBRARIES

Music Libraries

INCLUDING A COMPREHENSIVE BIBLIOGRAPHY
OF MUSIC LITERATURE AND
A SELECT BIBLIOGRAPHY OF MUSIC SCORES
PUBLISHED SINCE 1957

Original edition by Lionel Roy McColvin
and Harold Reeves

Completely re-written, revised and extended by
Jack Dove
F.L.A., F.R.C.O., A.R.C.M.
Borough Librarian and Curator of Hove

VOLUME ONE

ANDRE DEUTSCH
A GRAFTON BOOK

FIRST PUBLISHED 1965 BY
ANDRE DEUTSCH LIMITED
105 GREAT RUSSELL STREET
LONDON WC1
COPYRIGHT © 1965 BY JACK DOVE

PRINTED IN GREAT BRITAIN BY
EBENEZER BAYLIS AND SON LIMITED
WORCESTER AND LONDON

Music Libraries by Lionel R. McColvin and Harold
Reeves was originally published by Grafton & Co.
in 1937. This edition has been fully revised and
re-written by Jack Dove

Preface

Twentieth-century British librarianship is indebted more to Lionel Roy McColvin than to any other person for dynamic leadership and an infectious enthusiasm. He commenced his career in Croydon and after service in Wigan and Ipswich he became Chief Librarian of the Hampstead Public Libraries in 1931. By this time, still only 35, he had written textbooks on Extension Work and Publicity, and Book Selection.

In 1924, however, he had produced *Music in Public Libraries*, his first publication, which was in fact his librarianship diploma thesis. Since then he has written twenty books, most of them concerned with the business of librarianship in all its various facets.

In 1937, thirteen years after its first appearance and a year before he became City Librarian of Westminster, he and Harold Reeves, a music publisher, bookseller and bibliographer, produced the second edition of *Music Libraries*, which now became a two-volume work. The first volume concerned itself with the organization and contents of music collections in public libraries, with a bibliography of music and musical literature. The second volume had a comprehensive classified list of music and notes on collections and libraries of music and music literature all over the world. Lionel McColvin was particularly suited to this specialized subject, as not only was he a fine librarian, he was also an accomplished musician.

Harold Reeves started in business on his own at 210 Shaftesbury Avenue, London, W.C.2, in 1919. Twenty years later he transferred his business to Bournemouth and in 1946 sold it to Kenneth Mummery. He was passionately fond of music and gave five prizes at various times after the War for orchestral compositions. He died on February 8, 1961.

Soon after publication of the McColvin and Reeves *Music Libraries* came the Second World War, with its wholesale disruptions of existing services in local government, not least the library service. For McColvin, however, the débâcle provided a challenge. This

was the time for a review of the public library service of Great
Britain and for proposals directed towards its reorganization and
improvement. He produced the McColvin Report in 1942. McColvin was not to be satisfied however. He went on writing, speaking,
directing and advising on library affairs, not only at home but
abroad, and somehow found the time to produce more books,
despite his appointment as City Librarian of Westminster.

As I write, this industrious, much-loved man has been compelled
to retire owing to a sudden breakdown in health and it is a pleasure,
as well as a privilege to me, to have been entrusted with a revision of
Music Libraries.

In his excellent, comprehensive treatise, *Music Librarianship*,
E. T. Bryant freely admitted his immense debt to the earlier editions
of this work, stressed the influence they had exerted in Britain and
the U.S.A. and commended particularly the chapter on cataloguing
and McColvin's own alteration of Dewey as an alternative system of
classification. The tables are now reversed. Music in libraries is a
field which was largely ignored from 1937 until Eric Bryant issued
his mammoth work in 1959 and to his textbook I make grateful
acknowledgment. It seemed obvious that the duplication of entries
for standard music scores would be wasteful. Bryant covered the
ground so thoroughly and made such liberal annotations, that I
decided to make my bibliography a selective list of music published
since 1957. This is a personal selection and there are, of course,
many omissions, particularly of orchestral items. Nevertheless, it
should help in the choice of music published recently which in my
view should find a place in all but the smallest libraries. Whilst I
have tried to adhere to the content of the original work as nearly as
possible, there have been obvious necessitous changes and doubtless
many omissions. I shall therefore welcome criticisms and suggestions
for any possible future re-issue.

Jack Dove

Acknowledgments

To undertake the revision of a textbook of this kind in such a rapidly developing artistic field, was an undertaking of far greater magnitude than I contemplated when I accepted the invitation from Messrs. André Deutsch. Consequently, although it has taken me two years, I could not have completed it without help on all sides.

I therefore thank all those librarians, at home and overseas, who showed tolerance in having yet another questionnaire to complete. Especially am I indebted to those who sent me much fuller information than the form provided for, in addition to copies of catalogues and various printed publications. The librarians of the Central Music Library at Westminster excelled themselves. Not only were their printed publications put at my disposal but the premises as well, and to the City Librarian, Mr K. C. Harrison, M.B.E., F.L.A., Miss Joan Pemberton, M.A., A.L.A., now Mrs Smith, formerly Music Librarian, and Mr L. Sopher, M.A., F.L.A., the present librarian, I am particularly indebted.

The checking of the bibliographies was an arduous task, spreading itself over many months. In this connection, I could not have had a more painstaking, friendly ally than Mr A. Hyatt-King of the British Museum a well-renowned figure in music circles all over the world. Another equally popular and respected figure, Mr John H. Davies, F.L.A., B.B.C. Music Librarian, gave me much initial encouragement and explained in detail the ramifications of his organization.

Chapter 5 contains particulars of journals with musical interests and the many editors concerned sent me samples of their publications for which I owe a special thank you.

The arrangement of the bibliographies, their typing and their checking was shared between members of my own staff, and I have a large debt to them. Particularly would I mention Miss Dorothy E. Tunks, A.L.A.; Mrs V. J. Russell, A.L.A.; the Misses L. M. Green, A.L.A., P. E. Shaddock, C. Belmont, W. Boothroyd,

ACKNOWLEDGMENTS

J. M. Bosomworth and A. Dillistone. The typing of the manuscript was undertaken in part by Miss Doreen Lock, Mrs S. M. Mason and Miss Dorothy E. Tunks, and I am grateful to them.

Last but not least I owe a special acknowledgment to my wife and daughters, who have suffered an oppressed and persistent husband and father for many a long day.

Contents

Contents

Illustrations

Illustrations

I

General Survey of Musical Activity

THERE has been a spectacular growth of interest in music since 1945. The high standard of programmes produced by the British Broadcasting Corporation on sound and television and its Third Programme, aimed at the serious listener; a very noticeable awareness of the importance and value of music by educational authorities; and the advent of the long-playing record, of stereophonic sound and the new lease of life enjoyed by the gramophone, now styled by the more dignified title of a record player. These, I believe, are the three influential factors. Let us examine each in a little more detail.

Broadcasting is sometimes compared to the discovery of printing which brought a new stage in civilization by the making of many books and by the consequent spread of ideas and knowledge. The growth of broadcasting, which has been entirely a discovery and development of the twentieth century, has been like a revolution. Everybody, almost everywhere, is played upon by a constant stream of sounds bringing entertainment and news, events as they happen, music, politics and teaching. In the late 1920s and early 1930s, academic people had no use for the wireless but in the 1950s and 1960s, statesmen and rulers of the world appear frequently on the television screen, and dons speak regularly on the Third Programme. We take these marvels for granted, so rapidly have they come upon us, and been extended and elaborated.

In Britain, in 1919, a member of the Marconi company transmitted good speech from Ballybunion in Ireland to Louisburg, Cape Breton Island, a distance of 1,800 miles. A year later, two programmes of only half an hour each were put out from the new Chelmsford station and the *Daily Mail* became interested in them. So, Madame Melba broadcast and most European countries heard it. Wireless programmes had begun. In 1922, the 2LO station began

to broadcast from London, 2ZY from Manchester and the British
Broadcasting Company was formed, licensed by the Postmaster
General until 1926.

Official broadcasting by the B.B.C. began on November 14, 1922
with the declaration of the results of the general election. Right from
the start, the B.B.C., through its general manager, J. C. W. Reith
(later Sir John) had as its aims, the promotion of information, culture
and entertainment. In 1927 it became the British Broadcasting
Corporation and its aims have been constant.

By the end of the twenties broadcasting had laid the foundations
of lasting contributions to the culture of our time. The Corporation
had taken over and ensured the future of the Sir Henry Wood
Promenade Concerts: the B.B.C. Symphony Orchestra was about
to come into being: the *Listener*, partly as a result of the findings of
the Hadow Committee on Adult Education, had made its first
appearance: and school broadcasting was growing on a solid basis
of consultation and co-operation with the educational world. Then,
two thousand schools were using broadcasts: now the figure is
around thirty thousand.

Young children were of special concern and on suggestions made
by the H.M.I. Music Panel and by the staff of St. Katharine's
Training College, Ann Driver carried out a series of experiments in
music teaching at the Colindale Junior School, Hendon, and in
1934 launched her first 'Music and Movement' programmes for
children between the ages of 5 and 7. This, too, was the time of those
unforgettable broadcasts by Sir Henry Walford Davies. He first did
a series 'Music and the ordinary listener' from 1926 to 1929, and in
1940, commenced a further series 'Everyman's music' which lasted
about a year.

Wartime brought more broadcasts to schools, especially of orchestral performances, and then, in 1952, a pilot run of twenty television closed circuit programmes was broadcast and received in six
Middlesex schools. By 1957, the School Broadcasting Council had
become fully operational in television as well as in sound.

Early in that year, however, the sound broadcasting services were
rearranged owing to the growing popularity of television. The Third
Programme was reduced from $5\frac{1}{2}$ to 3 hours a night, the Home and
Light Programmes were combined at certain periods, and there was
to be a longer continuous service of light background music and
entertainment.

The Third Programme was started by Sir William Haley in 1946. It was aimed at a minority audience estimated at between 45,000 and 100,000 and was to bring to their ears a constant flow of all that is best, new and old, in music, literature and drama, in addition to topical talks on vital subjects. The cutting down of the length of time allotted to the programme inevitably meant that not so much little-known music was to be heard and consequently fewer younger composers were broadcast. New talent did not therefore receive as much encouragement, but it has been able to broadcast the classics, much early music not heard anywhere else, and new British operas, together with complete performances of great works such as Wagner's *Ring* relayed from Bayreuth. In the tenth anniversary celebration programmes of the Third Programme, nine new works were specially commissioned from contemporary composers.

Sound radio is still the principal medium for the broadcasting of music of all kinds and 40 per cent of the B.B.C.'s sound output is in fact of music. As an artistic patron, too, the B.B.C. has a high repu-tation. It has the necessary funds and an appreciative, well-informed, critical understanding of what musicians try to achieve. In 1961 alone, thirty-seven compositions were given world premières, one hundred and twenty-five were broadcast for the first time and there were forty broadcasts of works never previously performed in the United Kingdom. At midday on a Sunday in that year, $12\frac{1}{2}$ million people listened to 'Two-way Family Favourites'. No other agency, therefore, has this enormous potential and its effects are now taken for granted by all Britishers. The home would be a poorer, deathly place without the radio.

Vision limits the mind and slows down comprehension. Be that as it may, it is exciting and brings events of magnitude into one's very living-room. B.B.C. television began in 1936 at Alexandra Palace and not until June 1960 did it acquire a studio specifically designed for television production. This came with the opening of the Television Centre, the largest building of its kind in the world.

In 1954, commercial or independent television was established by Act of Parliament. These manifold channels of entertainment and education between them provide something for everyone. And for the musician, exchanges of music, opera, drama and light enter-tainment have followed the agreement between the European Broadcasting Union and the International Federation of Musicians.

The second reason I have cited for the post-war growth of interest in music is the enlightened attitude of education authorities. At last music has taken its place in the schools and colleges. It is no longer looked upon as the poor relation of the arts, although the place it occupies largely depends upon the musical interest of the head or principal. A non-musical person can still relegate the study of music to the dinner-hour, and to already over-full after-school activities, whilst the performances of school choir and orchestra, if they do in fact exist, are a necessary evil.

Specialists are appointed to school staffs, and many counties have their musical advisers, who hold a watching brief over the musical activities of publicly maintained schools. Local education authorities vote money for specific purposes such as the purchase of scores and parts, of instruments and records. They organize concerts and holiday schools, and provide library facilities, which include the provision of instrumental scores, vocal scores, part songs and orchestral parts, miniature scores, gramophone records and textbooks. The established colleges are getting away from the narrow training of performers and insisting upon all-round ability and intensive knowledge, both linguistic and historical. The universities have established new departments and are experimenting.

All this is the due of the present-day student. The man who hears and listens has as many opportunities as the man who sees or reads. He may have more, for classical music easily satisfies the emotional and aesthetic needs of many people today. Music has its own literature and its own history. Its composition follows certain technical rules and patterns – more extensive and varied, I would suggest, than those for poetry, drama or storytelling. The imaginative demands are no less exacting and deep set. Why then should this major art be treated in a subservient, casual way?

The Ministry of Education itself is giving a lead, long overdue, as indeed it should for music is all around every one of us. It is the accompaniment to everyday life, more subtle, more influential and more insistent that many other of the so-called fine arts. Many are the concert and opera goers; many more belong to amateur choirs and orchestral societies; a large number are collectors of records and scores; and listeners can be counted by the thousand. I would wager that the number of adults who enjoy good music after their schooldays is greater than that of those who enjoy good literature and the visual arts.

Even so, the number of children who take music at ordinary level in the G.C.E. is still small. For every one, there are twenty who take literature and nine who take art. Overall, 1 in 200 take music at O-level and 1 in 170 at A-level – low proportions indeed from $1\frac{1}{2}$ million children who sit G.C.E. each year. The percentage of passes is high however: 68 per cent at O-level and 72 per cent at A-level. The small numbers taking music are entirely due to the lack of recognition in the past by the Ministry of Education of music as a serious academic subject. Now this day has passed. Nevertheless, the needs of classroom music are still overlooked. The hall, when not in use, or the dining-hall will suffice for the musician. This is not good enough. There should be special accommodation for piano, instruments, record player and radio, with sufficient storage space for music scores and music stands.

However, our best chances of promoting music as an O-level subject lie in emphasizing the historical aspect. In the history of music, we have a story of unique value because it is the story of creation; positive not negative, constructive not destructive. We have in our hands, one of the only unifying forces in the world today. Musicians of all nations are able to work together in a high degree of harmony. Never before has so much music been poured out each day into the ears of the world. What a challenge to teachers in schools!

Finally, consider art which was so definitely the Cinderella subject, at least in boys' schools, thirty years ago. Why is it that many more pupils submit art at O-level than music? Probably because of parental pressure. Art is creative as is music, but music is looked upon by many parents as an out-of-school activity, or relaxation. It is necessary to sell music to parents as well as pupils, and this is no mean task![1]

Dr J. H. Alden, Secretary of the Music Masters Association, believes that the present-day place of music in education, especially its growth in state schools, has resulted from seed sown in the minds of education officials who themselves passed through boarding schools as schoolboys. He cited[2] Paul David (Uppingham 1865–1907); John Farmer (Harrow 1862–1885); Eaton Faning (Harrow 1885–1901); Basil Johnson (Rugby 1886–1892, Eton 1892–1926); Edward Sweeting (Rossall 1882–1897, Winchester 1901–1924); and Clement Spurling (Oundle 1891–1936). Sir Henry Hadow writing

---

[1] William E. May, 'Controversy at O level', *Times Literary Supplement*, March 2, 1962, p. 398.
[2] *Times Literary Supplement*, March 2, 1962, p. 395.

on music at most Public Schools in the mid-19th century said : "the reluctant substitute for cricket, all the more bitter because it carried a suspicion of unmanly performance; the hours of drudgery to which no intelligible aim was propounded; the lack of discipline and authority; the whole subject regarded as alien and superfluous, commonly treated with a sort of disdainful toleration, but not admitted within the customary frontiers of citizenship." These sentiments were true, in my case, in the year 1932, in a grammar school with an ex-army officer as its head!

The Schools Music Association in its 1962 report on Music in Secondary Schools says that only two out of every three secondary schools have one full-time music specialist and that 177 of the 343 schools from whom they had replies have between 500 and 800 pupils. Their questionnaire was in fact addressed to 830 schools in 10 different areas and less than half replied. The Chairman of the Association believes that industry and professions insisting on O-levels and A-levels in the G.C.E. are aggravating the position of educational specialization and that music takes fourth or fifth place in academic subjects. Music activity out of school hours, however, is prodigious with school orchestras and choirs in abundance. This report emphasizes the need for the recognition of music as an academic subject, and stresses that it should not be treated as a leftover or as the abnormal child's pursuit.

Only one in three of our grammar schools has music as a compulsory subject in the curriculum at all stages in the school. In 20 per cent of our grammar schools, it is never a compulsory subject and where it is, the number of periods allotted to it are few. This again points to the heads of the schools. They must be converted to a practical belief that something is lacking in their schools if music does not play a vital part. The initiative must come from them. To plead to not being musical is a poor excuse: the scientist can hardly be a historian, or the arts degree person a chemist. But history and chemistry are assured of a place in the curriculum.

Much, too, depends on the staff. The possession of a music degree in itself is no guarantee of that vitality and inventiveness which are necessary to put the subject over adequately. A bachelor of music may be a fine theoretician but this degree gives no guarantee of practical musicianship. His ability to transpose, to sight read and to play from a full score may be non-existent. Nor does it mean that he can inspire a class with musical enthusiasm. And if this were not enough, patience and discipline are also demanded of the music teacher. The pre-war idea of a music lesson in school was an hour's singing, usually loathed or regarded as wasteful, by the majority. Now, at last, it means much more. Singing, yes; but also listening and appreciation, theory and aural training. And the history and development of music needs to be set against the social and political conditions of the time. That Handel, in fact, was writing when Walpole was towards the end of his Premiership, Voltaire was writing in France and John Wesley had started his Methodist revival : or that Chopin was attaining his peak when public education was to become a fait accompli, when Victoria was about to be Queen and Dickens was active in exposing the appalling social conditions in the country.

The requirement of Grade V of the music conservatoires examinations for music at O-level in the General Certificate of Education and of Grade VI for A-level is a wise one. With some universities these are alternatives to theory and aural papers : London University demands Grade VI from A-level candidates. Trinity College and the Guildhall School demand G.C.E. qualifications for their teaching diplomas.[1] At least, these do guarantee a certain standard of practical attainment. Since the war, the encouragement of instrumental music by education authorities has been most noticeable and over two-thirds of our maintained grammar schools now provide instrumental tuition of some kind.

There is also the welcome development of rural music schools for playing in ensemble. We read of percussion groups in the primary schools : of the teaching of the recorder as the next introduction to music, helpful as it is in the study of musical notation, tempo and rhythm : and of orchestras in the secondary schools. Too often, they have to meet in the dinner hour, or after school, an impossibility for children in rural areas who have a long bus ride each day. Boarding schools have a distinct advantage in this direction of course.

Many grammar schools have music societies which indulge in group listening, well-known personalities to lecture, and pay visits to orchestral, operatic and choral concerts.

[1] Grades V and VI (Intermediate) Examinations, Associated Board of the Royal Schools of Music.
Grades V and VI (Senior) Examinations, Trinity College of Music.
Grade VI Examinations, London College of Music.
Grade VI Examinations, Guildhall School of Music.

Degree courses at English universities fall into two groups: those in which music is the main subject of study, namely the Bachelor of Music and the Bachelor of Arts in Music; and those in which music is taken with other subjects of equal or greater importance, namely the Bachelor of Arts General Studies. The university music department is usually small: the degree courses are similar. They include harmony, counterpoint, orchestration and composition with a general knowledge of musical history including a special period and in some cases, set works.

Honours Schools of music are now established in more than half the English universities – evidence of the academic recognition of music.

I am sure I am right in stating that the various colleges of music now have more pupils than ever. The Royal Academy of Music has 750; the Royal College of Music 466; Trinity College 600; the London College of Music 500; the Guildhall School of Music and Drama 1,600; the Royal Scottish Academy of Music 1,000; the Birmingham School of Music 720; and the Royal Manchester College of Music 325.

No minimum educational qualifications are demanded. Entry is dependent on an audition and sometimes a theoretical examination. A certain technique is essential here. On the other hand, a lack of inspiration and genuine feeling for music, which may not be apparent at the time of entry, will prove a handicap later on. They tend to produce 'mechanical musicians'.

In his fascinating reminiscences *My Record of Music*, Sir Compton Mackenzie, quite naturally, had much to say about the gramophone. "There is no question at all that the effect on music is going to be entirely beneficial. For my own part, I believe that we are moving toward a point of human development when it will only be possible to express in music the complicacy of modern emotion. The great obstacle in the way of music has always been the difficulty of obtaining it. It is pathetic to think that an inadequate instrument like the piano should have represented practically the whole of the mechanical facilities which music received during a hundred years of mechanical progress in every direction. And when, finally, the gramophone arrived, it was allowed to remain perfectly unprogressive by those who exploited it. As usual, the public was blamed, and we were told that the public did not want good music and that they would not buy good records. It is hardly necessary to point out that this was all nonsense, for as soon as the gramophone companies began to provide good music in sufficient quantity, they found not merely that wireless, their mighty new competitor, was not going to ruin them, but that it was actually going to help them."

He went on to say that "there is no reason why in another fifty years, it should not be possible to find libraries of music that will compare with the great libraries of literature today. Let the recording companies take warning from the history of publishing: let them note that no great publishing business has ever been built up by publishing rubbish, even if a brief prosperity has deluded some firms into supposing that a pander's life is longer than the wares he sells."

The gramophone was invented in 1877 by Thomas Edison, and Alexander Bell put his first cylindrical machine on the market in 1889. It has had a variable history. In the 1930s it was as dead as a dodo. The records had changed from the cylindrical to the one-sided disc and thereafter to the disc pressed on both sides and revolving at 78 r.p.m. After the Second World War, in 1950, came the long-playing record and with it a revolution in the record industry. Here was high fidelity recording with a playing time of an hour on a double-sided unbreakable microgrooved disc revolving at $33\frac{1}{3}$ r.p.m. The reproducing equipment was improved out of all recognition and in the late 1950s came stereophonic sound.

The famous Electrical Music Industries research engineer, A. D. Blumlein, had completed equipment for making and reproducing disc stereo recordings as early as 1931. By 1954, Arthur Haddy of Decca developed and perfected equipment for making and reproducing stereo records commercially and in 1957 John Moseley started to work at laboratories in Denmark on behalf of Pye records. By April 1958, he had succeeded in transcribing stereo tapes to discs and Pye were the first company in the world to have stereo records on sale to the public. Stereo records from Decca and E.M.I. followed five months later. Thus two independent channels were recorded in a single groove of a disc record, one on each wall, on the 45/45 principle.

Another development is that of recorded tapes costing twice as much as the dearest l.p. 12-inch record which sells at 48s 4d. The Electrical Music Industries group began selling tapes of music at the Radio Show in 1954. Tape recorders are common to many homes and the playing of tapes at lower speeds than the long-playing record gives them decided advantages. In addition, if they break they can be mended and deterioration is not a drawback. Tape recordings are used extensively by the broadcasting companies and the quality of reproduction is good. Storage of them presents fewer problems than do records.

56½ million long-playing records were sold in the U.K. in 1960 and 70 million long-playing records were produced, 14 million of them 33⅓ r.p.m. and 56 million 45 r.p.m. Gramophone clubs flourish and record recitals are a popular extension activity of many public libraries. Record clubs bring first-class recordings to their members at reduced prices and there are the cheap price series put out by the big companies such as Decca's 'Ace of Clubs', Pye's 'Golden Guinea' and the Heliodor series.

All over the country, there is evidence of an upsurging in musical interest and activity. This fact emerges from the reports of the Arts Council, the established patron of all the arts.

The Council was formed on August 9, 1946 and its growth has been phenomenal. Its Charter of Incorporation states that its aim is "for the purpose of developing a greater knowledge, understanding and practice of the fine arts exclusively and in particular to increase the accessibility of the fine arts to the public throughout our Realm, to improve the standard of execution of the fine arts and to advise and co-operate with our Government Departments, local authorities and other bodies on any matters concerned directly or indirectly with those objects, and with a view to facilitating the holding of and dealing with any money provided by Parliament and any other property, real or personal, otherwise available for those subjects. . . ."

There are five permanent symphony orchestras associated with the Arts Council – the City of Birmingham Symphony, the Bournemouth Symphony, the Hallé, the Royal Liverpool Philharmonic and the Scottish National. Between them, they give over one thousand concerts per year. The London Philharmonic and the London Symphony orchestras are associated with the Council for specific concert promotions, and tangible encouragement is also given to other orchestras including the Brighton Philharmonic, the Northern Sinfonia and the Lemare Orchestra. A Society for the Promotion of New Music and the Music Section of the Institute of Contemporary Arts are affiliated to the Arts Council and arrange vitalizing programmes.

The number of societies affiliated to the National Federation of

Music Societies is now eight hundred, and these include chamber music clubs, choral and orchestral societies. Amateur societies are active too with their productions of oratorios and operas.

Music festivals are held in large cities and in small towns alike from Leeds, Croydon and St Pancras on the one hand, to Orpington and Worthing on the other. Smaller festivals include those at Warwick, Dawlish, St Bees, Tilford and Mickleham.

Opera and ballet are no less in the ascendancy. In 1960–1 Sadler's Wells used its two permanent companies of equal strength to provide forty-three weeks of opera and operetta *outside* London. The Welsh National Opera Company provides six weeks of opera in Welsh cities and makes an annual visit to Sadler's Wells. And of course there is the Royal Opera House at Covent Garden with its stupendous programmes and its magnificent settings. I cannot resist mentioning what is, in my view, the most exciting venture of all. The economic conditions of the past generation have hardly been conducive towards private enterprise in this field, but Mr John Christie[1] at Glyndebourne in the rolling Sussex downs, has proved what foresight, determination and a shrewd artistic sense can achieve. He built the Glyndebourne Festival Opera House in 1934. He had married a singer, Audrey Mildmay and from her he learned to appreciate opera. Now, opera-goers from all over the world come to hear and see operas, old and new, performed perfectly in the intimate theatre which seats a mere six hundred.

The Association Internationale des Bibliothèques Musicales was founded in Paris in 1950 under the auspices of Unesco. Its address is 14 rue de Madrid, Paris 8, and its General Secretary M. V. Féderov. It has observers from Unesco: the International Music Council; the International Federation of Associations of Libraries; the International Federation for Documentation and the International Musicological Society. A United Kingdom Branch was founded on March 23, 1953, its threefold objects being to:

(1) provide a platform for the discussion of all matters affecting music libraries;
(2) stimulate interest in musical bibliography;
(3) encourage co-operation in all branches of musical librarianship.

The Royal School of Church Music founded in 1927 is situated

[1] Died July 4 1962.

in Addington Palace, Croydon, the erstwhile country residence of
the Archbishop of Canterbury, which became the headquarters of
the school in 1954. It is the centre of Church music for the Anglican
Communion throughout the world and has almost four thousand
affiliated choirs. It has a full-time course lasting one year but many
other courses are arranged, including weekend courses. The School
houses the library of Dr H. C. Colles, eminent musicologist, which
contains secular as well as sacred music not exclusively connected
with the Anglican Church.

The Canadian Music Centre is a non-profit making organization
and was formed in 1959. Its primary purpose is to make Canadian
music better known. It acts as a library and promoting agency for
the Canadian composer; is an information centre for music in
Canada and distributes published and manuscript scores by Canadian composers to conductors, performers and programme builders
for perusal, study and performance. The formation of the Music
Centre was largely due to the isolation of composers in a country
which stretches 4,000 miles from coast to coast and has only about
18 million population. The Centre receives a grant from the Canadian Music Council of $20,000 per year and the Composers,
Authors and Publishers Association of Canada Ltd, has regularly
matched half the Council's grant so far. It reproduces scores from
the composer's transparencies at no cost to the composer and sometimes engages professional copyists. The Library has over 2,500
works: several hundred tapes of broadcast performances and a
complete set of recordings issued by the International Service of the
C.B.C. In addition to the library of reproduced scores, a project
was started in 1960 of issuing eleven printed study or miniature
scores in quantities of three hundred for distribution. At present,
forty scores of Canadian compositions by seven publishers are available. As a study project for composition courses at universities and
conservatories, the Centre has arranged its first study course which
contains a taped analysis of his work by each composer represented
on the first Columbia recording. These analyses are published in
brochure form complete with musical excerpts. The latest project
is the commissioning of graded educational music towards which a
grant of $10,000 has been made by the Canada Council. A cata-
logue of orchestral music is at present in preparation.

2

Periodicals and Catalogues

WHAT then, in the light of all this activity, is the effect on public libraries? It means that in all but the smallest places recourse should be possible to a good, representative music collection. Such a collection would contain books on music, its history, its techniques, its composers and its instruments. Periodicals with musical aims should be provided and these are many. Naturally, only a selection can be taken but the following are the more important.

The British Catalogue of Music was first available in 1957 for an annual subscription of £4. It is now published three times a year. It is intended to be a permanent record of published British music. In addition, it records foreign music available in the United Kingdom through a sole agent and books about music. It is based on the works deposited at the British Museum where copies of all new publications must be sent under the Copyright Act. The publishers are the Council of the British National Bibliography Limited and it is issued in parts, with a bound volume annually. The first section is alphabetical by composer, title, arranger, editor, subject, form, series and instrument. It is, in fact, an index to the second section which is classified according to voices, instruments and combinations. It contains a section of musical literature. Prices of individual items are given and there is an index of music publishers and their addresses. A typical entry reads like this:

LUIGINI, Alexandre
 Ballet Egyptian themes; adapted and arranged by Jack Helyer [for] brass band. [Conductor and parts.] London, Lawrence Wright, 7s 6d. c. 1956. 19 pt. 8vo.

Accordion Times. Incorporates *Harmonica News* and *Modern Musician.* Editorial at Somerset House, Cranleigh, Surrey. Monthly 1s.

Established 1935. Notes of Music Festivals; of the British College of Accordionists and their examinations; feature articles.

Audio and Record Review. Hanover Press Ltd, 31 St George Street, London, W.1. Editor: Leonard Hibbs. 2*s* 6*d* monthly. Subscription £2 per annum. Incorporates the *Gramophone Record* which was founded by Leonard Hibbs in 1933, and *Record Review*. Has articles of general musical interest and a very extensive review coverage of new records, in addition to reports on recording equipment and reviews of new books. In a generous format and well illustrated.

B.M.G. Monthly. Editor: A. P. Sharpe at 20 Earlham Street, London, W.C.2. 1*s* 3*d*. Established 1903. Devoted to banjo, mandolin, guitar and kindred instruments. Record and book reviews; music inset; articles; correspondence columns.

Bärenreiter News. The first volume of the *Bärenreiter News* came in June 1962. It is a counterpart in English to the *Bärenreiter Bote* – a house journal in the German language. The firm of Bärenreiter in Kassel is well known in the musical world and the *News* in its present format gives particulars of new publications, both of music and of the Bärenreiter Musicaphon Records. The British agents are Novello and Company Ltd.

The Braille Musical Magazine published by the Royal National Institute for the Blind at 224 Great Portland Street, W.1. Monthly 6*d*. Topical information of interest to blind musicians, teachers and students of music, and pianoforte tuners. Carries reviews of new musical publications and compositions.

The British Bandsman. Bandsman's Press, 210 Strand, London, W.C.2. Editor: Eric Ball. Weekly 4*d*. Has reviews of gramophone records; details of brass band broadcasts; a band contest diary; correspondence columns and reports from district correspondents at home and activities abroad.

The Choir. The Choir Office, 25–35 City Road, London, E.C.1. Editor: J. Alan Kay, M.A., Ph.D. 1*s* 3*d* monthly. Subscription 17*s* 6*d* per annum. Is concerned with vocal music, sacred and secular, and with the organ and its music.

The Dance Band and Jazz Musician. Formerly the *Amateur and Semi-pro Musician*. Editor: Gordon Woolf, 305 High Street, Ponders End,

Enfield, Middlesex. Bi-monthly 6*d*. Founded November 1960. The modern dance music scene.

English Church Music. First published in 1928, as a news-sheet and in its present format in 1931. Royal School of Church Music, Addington Palace, Croydon, Surrey. Published three times a year in February, June and October. 2*s* per issue. Subscription 6*s* per annum. The official publication of the Royal School of Church Music. Carries reviews of music and musical literature.

Fontes Artes Musicae. Editorial offices: rue de Madrid, Paris VIIIe. Editor: Vladimir Fédorov. The half-yearly journal of the International Association of Music Libraries. Articles in English, French and German on the technical and bibliographic aspects of music librarianship. Contains a classified section of music and music literature published in the member countries, arranged in alphabetical order of country and thereafter under five main subject headings: (1) Theatre and Films; (2) Instrumental; (3) Vocal; (4) Folklore; (5) Music Literature.

The Gilbert and Sullivan Journal. Published for the Gilbert and Sullivan Society by Derek G. Hyde, 19a Lissenden Mansions, Lissenden Gardens, London, N.W.3. Three times a year – 1*s* 6*d* per issue. Carries notes on current productions of the operas; has slight correspondence columns; articles of reminiscences and news of G. and S. Branches at home and abroad.

Gramophone. First published 1923 by Sir Compton Mackenzie. 379 Kenton Road, Kenton, Harrow, Middlesex. Editors: Cecil Pollard and Anthony Pollard. Monthly 1*s* 6*d*. Incorporates *Vox*, *The Radio Critic* and *Broadcast Review*. Extensive advertisements. Excellent book reviews and reviews of new records under subject heads, such as Orchestral Music; Chamber Music; Instrumental; Choral and Song; Operatic; Humorous; Poetry and Diction. There are also reviews of classical reissues, with a section headed Miscellaneous, and Dance covering pop records, stage and screen, Latin-American and Continental. Swing and jazz notes take much space and classified advertisements complete this comprehensive and most reliable journal.

Guitar News. From Wilfrid M. Appleby, 47 Clarence Street, Cheltenham. Bi-monthly. On private subscription as a foundation member for 21*s* per annum; supporting member 15*s* or ordinary member 10*s* 6*d*. The official organ of the International Classic Guitar Association, a non-profit making, cultural organization, which fosters the better understanding and appreciation of the classic (Spanish) guitar. The journal contains articles on guitars and guitarists; gives information about music for the guitar and has articles on guitar playing and news of recitals. It is well illustrated.

Hi-Fi News. Editor: Miles Henslow. Editorial office: 99 Mortimer Street, London, W.1. 2*s* monthly. Subscription 27*s* 6*d* per annum. Incorporates *Tape and Tape Recorders, Audio News* and *Stereo News*. A technical magazine concerned with hi-fi and recording equipment, well illustrated, with reviews of new equipment.

Hit Parade. Hit Parade Publications Ltd, 23 Denmark Street, London, W.C.2. Monthly 2*s*. Plenty of illustrations; record reviews; notes of the day's stars and 'top pops'. Published since 1955.

Jazz Journal. Editor: Sinclair Traill, The Cottage, 27 Willow Vale, London, W.12. 2*s* 6*d* monthly. Subscription 30*s* per annum. Britain's oldest Jazz magazine, with articles on the jazz scene and record reviews. High standard of format and illustrations.

Jazz Monthly. Editor: Albert J. McCarthy, East Hill, St Austell, Cornwall. 2*s* 9*d* monthly. Subscription 35*s* per annum. Well produced with reviews of records and books.

Jazz News. First published 1956. Editor: Ian McLean, 18 Carlisle Street, Soho Square, London, W.1. 9*d* weekly. Readership estimated at 40,000. Covers jazz, the fringes of jazz and influences by and on jazz. Sponsors new and struggling jazz bands and clubs. Rigidly excludes 'pop' and 'swing' items. Record reviews.

Liturgy. Editor: Rev. J. D. Crichton, 14 Priest Lane, Pershore, Worcestershire. Quarterly 3*s*. Annual subscription 13*s* 4*d*. The quarterly of the Society of St Gregory, with articles on the liturgy and related topics, notes and news columns and reviews of new publications.

Making Music. The official journal of the Rural Schools Music Association, Little Benslow Hills, Hitchin, Herts. Editor: Helen Wright. Appears three times a year. 1*s* 6*d* each issue. A distinguished looking journal, featuring music in its widest sense. Reviews of books on music and new music of all kinds, vocal, instrumental and gramophone records.

Music and Musicians. Hansom Books, 7 and 8 Hobart Place, Eaton Square, London, S.W.1. Editor: Frank Granville Barker. Monthly 2*s*. Articles on music and musical activities; reviews of new music; diaries of musical events in and out of London; and well illustrated.

Musical Events. Dennis W. Mayers Ltd, 13 Heath Drive, Hampstead, London, N.W.3. Editor: Michael Hadley. Monthly since 1946, 1*s* 6*d*. Subscription 21*s* per annum. Has a musical survey, short record and book reviews, and a calendar of musical events in the London area.

Musical Opinion and Music Trade Review. Editor: Laurence Swinyard, Minerva House, 26–27 Hatton Garden, London, E.C.1. Monthly 1*s* 6*d*. Subscription £1 per annum. Founded 1877. Its contents are divided into two parts: (*a*) general, (*b*) the organ world. Gramophone records and new music have liberal notices.

Music and Letters. Music and Letters Ltd, Alma Terrace, Allen Street, London, W.8. Editor: Eric Blom. Published by the Oxford University Press. Quarterly 6*s* 6*d*. Founded 1920. Scholarly articles, reviews of books published at home and abroad.

Musical Quarterly. Publishers: G. Shirmer Inc., 3 East 43rd Street, New York 17. Editor: Paul Henry Lang. Quarterly $1.25. Subscription $4 per annum. Founded 1915. Timely and historical articles of scholarship with biographical and analytical studies of contemporary composers. Contains a current chronicle of new music; a quarterly book list of new books of all countries and publications on microfilm and record and book reviews.

Music in Education. Editor: Gordon Reynolds, 160 Wardour Street, London, W.1. 1*s* 6*d* every other month. Subscription 11*s* per annum. New gramophone records, new miniature scores, and new music are written up and whilst addressed particularly to schools, it is a lively magazine of general interest.

Music Review. Editor: Geoffrey Sharp, 'Herons', Barnston, Dunmow, Essex. Publishers: W. Heffer & Sons Ltd, 3 and 4 Petty Cury, Cambridge. Quarterly: February, May, August, November, 12*s* 6*d*. Subscription 42*s* per annum. Another scholarly journal with articles on musical trends, composers and musical structure. Critical book reviews, lengthy and discerning reviews of music and gramophone records.

Musical Times. Published by Novello & Co. Ltd, 160 Wardour Street, London, W.1. Single copy 1s 6d. Annual subscription 23s. Founded in 1844. The format has recently been changed and the magazine has now a much more progressive look. It carries scholarly articles; reviews of books, records and music; obituary notices and has correspondence columns. The Royal College of Organists' official announcements appear here, and there is a diary of events in London. It is illustrated and has an inset of some new vocal composition, sacred or secular.

Music Teacher and Piano Student. Incorporates *The Music Student* and *The Musician*. Publishers: Evans Bros Ltd, Montague House, Russell Square, London, W.C.1. Price 2s monthly. Subscription £1 8s 6d per annum. Gramophone records are reviewed and so is new music, arranged alphabetically under publishing houses. Recently published piano music is categorized according to the Associated Board's grades.

Music Trades Review. Incorporates *The Talking Machine* and *Wireless Trade News*. Editor: J. Raymond Tobin at Boston House, 63–64 New Broad Street, London, E.C.2. Monthly 2s 3d. Established in 1877. The business side of music and music making, covering exhibitions; manufacture of instruments; radio, television and record players. There are reviews of gramophone records and new music with notes from music publishers. A high standard of production and well illustrated.

New Records. Francis Antony Ltd, East Hill, St Austell, Cornwall. Monthly 9d. Records listed under name of company or series and has an index.

Notes. Published by the Music Library Association Incorporated, Music Division, Public Library, Washington, D.C., U.S.A. Quarterly. $6.50 (members) per annum. $5.00 to non-members per annum or $1.35 per copy. In countries where the second-class mailing privilege does not apply, the dues of members are $7.00 and the subscription rate $5.50. The original Editor was Richard S. Hill, who died in 1961. There are reviews of musical literature, music and gramophone records of an unusually high standard, with an international list of new publications about music arranged under alphabetical order of country. The gramophone records are categorized as excellent, adequate and inadequate, and a key is provided to the journals in which the original reviews appeared. Similarly, reviews which give no clear assessment of the performances and recordings are also mentioned. They are listed under subjects and composers. A list of music received is also included which does not spurn current, rhythmic compositions and the journal is an essential bibliography for music libraries of any respectable size.

Opera. Editor: Harold Rosenthal, 6 Woodland Rise, London, N.10. Published monthly by Magazines and Publications Ltd., Rolls House, Breams Buildings, London, E.C.4. Single copy 2s 6d. Annual subscription 40s. Founded by the Earl of Harewood in 1950. Well produced, liberally illustrated and reviews the opera scene at large. Has reviews of books on music and operatic records. Also carries a calendar of Covent Garden Opera House, Sadler's Wells Theatre and Sadler's Wells Tours.

Organ. First published 1900. Editor: Laurence Swinyard. Publishers: Musical Opinion Ltd, 26–27 Hatton Garden, London, E.C.1. A quarterly review for its makers, its players and its lovers.

Pianomaker, Music and Radio Retailer. Monthly. Editor: Fred Grouback, 13 St George's Street, Hanover Square, London, W.1. Publishers: E. H. Wheeler Ltd, London, N.1. Single copy 2s 3d. Annual subscription £1 10s. Has slight reviews of music and records.

Quarterly Record of the Incorporated Association of Organists. Editor: Stainton de B. Taylor, Round House, Magazine Lane, Wallasey. 6d. A newsy periodical relating to organs and organists, with many advertisers and limited review space.

Record Collector. Editor: James F. E. Dennis, 61 Fore Street, Ipswich. Monthly 1s 6d. Annual subscription £1. For collectors of vocal recordings on disc and cylinder. Each issue has a biography, photograph, discography and usually a critical survey of the records of a famous singer. Limited review space.

Records and Recording. Hansom Books, 7 and 8, Hobart Place, Eaton Square, London, S.W.1. Editor: David Hunt. Monthly 2s. Excellently produced, has articles on varied musical subjects and items of interest, both technical and otherwise. Detailed reviews of recordings under opera, orchestral, chamber music, instrumental, vocal, poetry and drama with useful indexes under composers and names of recording companies. Well illustrated.

Records of the Month. Sinclair's Publications Ltd, 13 St George Street, Hanover Square, London, W.1. Monthly 1s 6d. Subscription 20s per annum. Listed in one alphabetical sequence under title with occasional entries under performers. Very uneven multilith. Has a list of record companies.

Die Reihe. First issued 1955. Editors: Herbert Einert and Karlheinz Stockhausen. A periodical devoted to developments in contemporary music. Limited availability in English translations.

R.C.M. Magazine. Royal College of Music, Prince Consort Road, London, S.W.7. Editor: Miss Diana McVeagh. Single copy 3s 6d. 12s 6d per annum. Founded 1904. A journal issued once a term for past and present students, and friends of the Royal College of Music. The official organ of the R.C.M. Union, a Society founded in 1906 of past and present pupils, the officers of the college and other invited persons. A house journal.

The Score. Score Publishing Co. Ltd, 2 Beaufort House, London, S.W.3. Editor: William Glock. Three times a year. 7s 6d per copy. Subscription 21s per annum. A scholarly, well-produced magazine with articles of topical and historical interest and notices of new music under 'News and Comments'.

The Strad. Publishers: J. H. Lavender & Co., 2 Duncan Terrace, London, N.1. Editor: E. W. Lavender. Monthly 9d. Founded 1890. Deals exclusively with subjects connected with the playing, collecting and making of the violin, viola, violoncello and double bass, and the illustration and description of instruments by old and modern makers of all nationalities. Reviews of music for strings and many advertisements. Carries illustrations.

The Royal Musical Association's Research Chronicle No. 1 has just reached me. It is published by the Association with the support of the Fellowes Memorial Fund and the Ralph Vaughan Williams Trust. This is a 107-page booklet in duplicated typescript, quarto in size and very well done in distinctive coloured covers. The editor, Thurston Dart, writing from Jesus College, Cambridge, comments that every musical scholar, during the course of his investigations, accumulates large quantities of musicological raw material – lists, indexes, catalogues, calendars, extracts from newspapers, new fragments of biographical information, and so on. Much of this material is of no enduring value, but some of it is of great importance. Certain sections may find their way into footnotes or appendices to a typescript, doctoral dissertation, yet such dissertations are unsuitable for publication as they stand. Consequently, the *R.M.A. Chronicle* is aimed at circulating some of the more worthwhile material brought to light during the course of such investigations, whether they are the result of a passionate hobby or whether they have been carried out at universities.

The first volume is a calendar of references to music in newspapers published in London and the provinces from 1660 to 1719 and has been compiled by Michael Tilmouth of the Department of Music in Glasgow University from papers mainly in the Burney Collection of the British Museum and of provincial newspapers in various British libraries. Locations of these are to be found in G. A. Cranfield's *Hand-list of English provincial newspapers and periodicals*, 1700–1760, published by the Cambridge University Press in 1952. The volume costs 16s and further publications are envisaged. The Secretary is Nigel Fortune at 44 Philip Victor Road, Handsworth, Birmingham 21.

Tape Recorder. Editor: Miles Henslow, 99 Mortimer Street, London, W.1. Monthly 1s 6d. Subscription 21s per annum. Contains articles on tape recording and news of tape-recording clubs.

Tape Recording. Editor: R. Douglas Brown, 7 Tudor Street, London, E.C.4. Fortnightly 1s 6d. News of shows, exhibitions and fairs, new products and club activities. Reviews tape records, mono and stereo.

Tempo. A quarterly review of modern music. Publishers: Boosey and Hawkes Ltd, 295 Regent Street, London, W.1. Editor: Donald Mitchell. Excellent standard of production but with limited space for music reviews.

Not a periodical, but the most important bibliography for British librarians, and indeed those overseas as well, is *The British Union Catalogue of Early Music*, edited by Edith B. Schnapper which was published by Butterworths Publications Ltd, in 1958 in two volumes. It is a record of the holdings of music published before

2

1800 in over one hundred British libraries. It is not confined to editions of British music, nor to British editions of works by European composers, for it includes a great quantity of pieces issued in many European countries from the earliest days of music printing.

Approximately 60 per cent of the whole comes from the British Museum and there are 55,000 entries in all, with a separate vocal index of over 10,000 titles. The catalogue therefore serves as an up-to-date guide to the British Museum's collections of early music.

As will be seen from the list of libraries' rarer holdings later in the book, early printed music is in a variety of institutions, some of it in the most unexpected places. The B.U.C.E.M. covers national, university, college, cathedral, and public libraries as well as those of the teaching colleges, and includes music in the usual sense of the word. Works of musical literature have been excluded. The following are to be found there:

(1) musical works;
(2) music printed in or issued as a supplement to books and periodicals;
(3) settings of liturgies when these bear the name of a composer or editor;
(4) psalters and hymnals which contain musical settings.

The International Inventory of Music Sources is a project sponsored jointly by the International Association of Music Libraries and the International Musicological Society. The purpose of the Inventory is to provide for the first time, a complete and systematic record of all musical sources, both in the Western and Oriental tradition, for all countries and all periods up to 1800. The project was commenced in 1960 and is expected to be completed by 1970. It should bring to light for study and performance, many unknown works as well as new sources for known works. It will be invaluable for the study of musical palaeography and bibliography, and for historical research.

The administration is organized by an international committee on which are represented a score or so of the most important countries concerned and is divided between two centres, one in Paris and the other in Kassel. The committee meets annually to discuss progress, finance and editorial problems. The Paris centre is situated in the Music Department of the Bibliothèque Nationale and is dealing with the material for the *classified series*. The Kassel centre works in conjunction with the Archive of German Musical History and is dealing with material for the *alphabetical series*.

The Inventory comprises two series: I. A classified series published by Henle Verlag of München; II. An alphabetical series published by Bärenreiter of Kassel. The music is divided into two series. The first consists of music of special types and periods catalogued according to categories as follows:

(1) *Manuscript*. Theory of music from the Carolingian era to 1400. Polyphonic music of the thirteenth to fifteenth centuries. Tropes and sequences. Byzantine.
(2) *Printed*. Books about music published before 1800. Music published in collections in two groups: 1525–1700; 1700–1800. Italian libretti published before 1800.
(3) *Manuscript and Printed*. Keyboard music. Tablatures for plucked stringed instruments.

Publication of these twelve volumes is expected to be completed by 1965. The second series is expected to run into twenty volumes and will comprise one alphabetical sequence of all music – manuscript or printed, complete or fragmentary, in score, parts or sheets, original or transcribed, which was written or published before 1800 and bears the name of a single composer or is attributable with certainty to a composer.

A national committee in the United Kingdom is sponsored by the Royal Musical Association but as has been noticed previously in this book, the U.K. is the only country in Europe or the Americas for which official or semi-official support for the Inventory has not been secured. Consequently, the cataloguing of manuscript music is likely to be a prolonged task.

3

Staff: Stock: Publishers and Booksellers

IN addition to the periodicals and catalogues mentioned in the previous chapter, miniature and pocket scores will be used by performer, teacher, critic, lecturer, student and listener alike, whilst a collection of actual scores knows no bounds. These will be in bound and sheet form and extensive duplication is practised in many libraries which provide orchestral parts, oratorios, cantatas, part-songs, anthems and operas. In addition, there should be gramophone records. Ninety-two British library authorities provide record collections and the earliest was established by the Middlesex County Libraries in 1935 for the use of schools. The University of London had a record library a little later for the use of students and the B.B.C. had an outstanding collection. The earliest record collection open to the general public was at the Chingford Branch of the Essex County Libraries in 1946 and collections were begun soon after at Walthamstow, Hampstead and Sutton Coldfield.

These show a desire to advance with the times and the treatment afforded to them shows a sense of responsibility and appreciation of this additional facility. Listening carrels are an essential, with record players controlled by the staff; modern retail shops have set the pace and some are magnificently equipped and stocked.

A separate music department, staffed by qualified personnel, is the ideal. Here books and other material, whether intended for lending or reference purposes, can be kept together and a truly efficient service given. After all, it is little short of foolish to have musical scores, textbooks and biographies in one department, with Groves' *Dictionary*, Clough and Cummings' *Recorded Music* and the like elsewhere.

Where this happens wastage and unnecessary duplication take place, and the available resources are never exploited to the full. Equally, I am sure that many an inquirer thereby leaves the library unsatisfied or dissatisfied. There are the musical rarities, such as early missals, autographed scores, original compositions in manu-script, autograph letters and in some cases, first editions which are intended for reference only. These are still capable of being kept and displayed in the music department, however, although more often than not, they must perforce be part of the reference collec-tions.

The provision of a piano or pianos is desirable in sound-proof cubicles, and if the library is fortunate enough to have a concert hall or lecture theatre, a grand piano will be essential.

Branch libraries can be provided with collections of music, the extent of the collection being dependent upon the size and type of area served, and the accommodation available. Obviously, dis-crimination must be exercised and only live items should appear on the shelves. It is no use allowing one's zeal and idealism to get the upper hand, and provide say Franz Liszt's *Piano Concertos*, Benjamin Britten's *Noyes Fludde*, Richard Strauss's *Death and Transfiguration* just because they are acknowledged classics. Such items will form part of the main collection kept at the central or county library headquarters, and be sent to the branches as and when required. The collection at the branch should be examined frequently, and new items substituted for those which are not being used.

Nor should children's libraries be overlooked. The young player, singer or dancer should have a choice of music, as generous as funds will permit. Instruction manuals or tutors for beginners: the annual publications of the Associated Board of the Royal Schools of Music; works for solo piano and piano duet; for recorder in solo form, duo, trio and quartet; for other solo instruments; song books; books of dances, including those of the Royal Academy of Dancing; hymnals and books of carols. All these will be used and used freely. The ability of the young should not be under-estimated.

I have already mentioned the need for qualified librarians in charge of music collections. I do not propose to enter into any protracted argument about librarian-*v.*-musician. Obviously, a librarian is the pre-requisite factor, for classification and cataloguing demand some thorough training and extensive practice. A librarian with some musical ability, experience and qualification is even more to be desired. The possession of a music degree or diploma presupposes a knowledge of the rudiments of the subject.

A degree implies specialist knowledge and this awareness of the manifold implications of the subject will amply reinforce the librarian in his dealings with the world and his wife. Additionally, there are those who listen much, read widely, have developed wide sympathies and taken pains to acquire some considerable knowledge of the history of the art, but who possess no musical qualifications as such. They are valuable folk and I can think of many amongst my acquaintances who would make fine music librarians with some training in librarianship.

After all, the duties of a person in charge of a music department are not confined to the four walls of his domain. He will attend and promote concerts and recitals; he will be called upon to give lectures and recital programmes; he may be required to prepare programme notes, and he will certainly mix with musical people of all kinds in his off-duty periods. Therefore, the greater his all-round ability, the greater the success of his library will be.

The financial rewards for such a person must be adequate. Nothing less than the National Joint Council's Administrative Salary Grade III is his minimum due, with a higher salary when the size of the department warrants it. Obviously, the person in charge at Hampstead will not have the stock and staff to control, nor the volume of inquiries, as the librarian in charge of the Henry Watson Library. Chief Librarians should not be chicken-hearted in establishing these gradings, especially in the light of the recent Burnham award to the teaching profession. A teacher in charge of music will have a maximum salary determinable by the type of training and qualifications. An honours graduate will have £1,460, a graduate will receive £1,300, and a non-graduate £1,200.

The provision of music, in its widest sense, is dependent upon one's own knowledge, the requirements of the area and a thorough working knowledge of bibliographical material. The Public Libraries Act of 1892 gave legal sanction for the provision of books, newspapers, maps and specimens of art and science. Music, record tapes and gramophone records are covered by this specimens clause.

Therefore, the question is, what to select? I have mentioned the British Catalogue of Music, which is a most useful source. Music publishers issue lists from time to time. Messrs. Ascherberg, Hopwood and Crew Ltd, 16 Mortimer Street, London, W.1, publish a catalogue of selected publications which is undated and arranged in order of title within broad subject headings. Their leaflets are many and range from accordion music to full scores for military bands.

Messrs. Augener Ltd, late of 18 Great Marlborough Street and now at 148 Charing Cross Road, London, W.C.2, are well known for the high standard and comprehensiveness of their publications. In the autumn of 1960 they issued their first *Augener News*, a half-yearly bulletin of recent publications. The summer 1961 *News* announced that they had absorbed A. Weekes & Co. Ltd, and the Challen Piano Co. Ltd, two internationally famous music houses, offering a wide range of musical instruments and equipment. The Augener Music-Supply Service aims at giving a service of music by return of post, no matter where or by whom published. The firm was established in 1853 and a catalogue of the Augener edition of classical music is issued on request.

Messrs. J. B. Cramer & Co., of 139 New Bond Street, London, W.1, have earned for themselves a fine reputation for their excellent service to libraries over many years. This is due to Mr H. P. Dawson, a modest, keen, well-informed sales manager, and an authority on musical publications. The *Library Music Bulletin* has appeared quarterly since 1947 and is a survey of British music publishing and agencies. The overseas subscription is 20*s* post free. It is a useful check list giving composer, title and price.

Cramer's have been famous in the library world over a long period for their bound albums of vocal, piano, organ, violin, violoncello, harp and guitar music. Their basic and standard music library list was last revised in January 1960, an extended version of their pre-war-list, *A music library for £100*. In 1957 they launched a scheme whereby the music of stage and films, arranged for piano, would be bound in annual volumes and, in fact, the first year covered was 1955. The firm undertakes the binding of music scores and is to be congratulated on the services it has given and continues to give to university, county and public libraries.

Novello & Co. Ltd, of 160 Wardour Street, London, W.1, also issue news bulletins irregularly. The firm has recently taken over the Edward Arnold Series of Music edited by Herbert Howells and also has become sole distributor of the Elkin edition. They issue various catalogues of choral, instrumental and vocal compositions, as well as seasonal lists and the Novello edition is well known to all musicians.

Another famous name in British music is Boosey and Hawkes Ltd, 295 Regent Street, London, W.1. Their catalogues are many, their pocket scores invaluable, and they are sole selling agents for the

Anglo-Soviet Music Press. Chappell, well known for their pianos, issued their first *Music News* in June 1961 and sadly failed to cite their address and telephone numbers. They are, of course, to be found at 50 New Bond Street, London, W.1, and they have entered the field of contemporary educational music publishing. Catalogues for piano, vocal and instrumental music are in process of publication and they will be followed by a full Education Catalogue. Items are graded according to difficulty and music teachers will find these lists of great value.

J. & W. Chester Ltd, 11 Great Marlborough Street, London, W.1, published *The Chesterian* quarterly, a small octavo-sized booklet carrying a few articles on a varied selection of musical topics and comments of new music. It was a chatty and informative magazine with a distinguished list of contributors from all over the world, but became defunct in the autumn of 1961.

Many reputable book publishers also publish music. Macmillan and Co. Ltd, St Martin's Street, London, W.C.2, have a growing list of publications of music and musical literature for schools. Their fame however rests largely on the monumental Grove and to a lesser extent, on such books as Sir Edward Bairstow's *Counterpoint and Harmony* and Cecil Forsyth's *Orchestration*, essential works for the advanced music student and the qualified musician.

The Oxford University Press issues three *Music Bulletins* per year, January to May, May to September and September to January, from their Music Department at 44 Conduit Street, London, W.1, which was established in 1923. The tercentenary of Oxford Music was celebrated on September 20, 1959 when a special pamphlet was issued entitled *Oxford Music 1659 to 1959* to mark the anniversary of the publication of a set of *Cheerfull Ayres or Ballads* by John Wilson, Doctor in Musick, Professor of the same in the University of Oxford. Seasonal lists come from time to time and a catalogue of Oxford music is published. The Press claims to be the largest publisher of sheet music in the country and probably the largest publisher of books about music in the world.

G. Ricordi & Co. Ltd, of 271 Regent Street, London, W.1, issue annual lists of new publications and reprints, and also have a selected catalogue covering their outstanding titles. Orchestral parts are available on hire for most of the songs and arias listed and the Ricordi classical miniature scores have earned commendation from many eminent contemporary musicians for their clarity, spacing, accuracy and pleasing appearance.

The catalogue of G. Schirmer Inc., the New York firm of music publishers and their library of musical classics is published by Chappell and Co., whilst the long-standing publishers Schott & Co. Ltd, of 48 Great Marlborough Street, London, W.1, also issue instrumental and vocal catalogues, which include miniature scores.

Music can be purchased at discount rates from appropriate dealers and in common with other items, its costs have mounted in recent years. It is well therefore, if a special sum is allocated to the music department for the purchase of necessary items. By this method alone can any attempt be made at balanced provision. Accessions should be constant and planned. There is no room for the haphazard and casual.

Second-hand sources should not be overlooked, although a chary attitude is essential here. Messrs. Holleyman and Treacher, Duke Street, Brighton, carry a large and varied stock, and are always willing to endeavour to obtain the out-of-the-way item. Kenneth Mummery of 9 St Winifred's Road, Bournemouth, issues the finest catalogues I have seen of music and musical literature. The new series of these publications has now reached catalogue No. 20. The entries are fully descriptive, the typography is faultless and they provide a veritable mine of information.

Musica Rara of 25 Newport Court, London, W.C.2, are also specialists in rare music and books on musical subjects and their lists are necessities for the music librarian. Otto Haas of 49a Belsize Park Gardens, London, N.W.3, issues fine catalogues of rare and out-of-the-way items.

The First Edition Bookshop of Cecil Hopkinson at 211 Abbey House, Victoria Street, London, S.W.1, issues music lists from time to time. These are elegantly produced and include rare items, mostly first editions, of scores and books on music, together with manuscripts, autograph letters and presentation copies of works by famous composers.

B. and L. Wilson Ltd, of 2 Warwick Mansions, Pond Street, Hampstead, London, N.W.3, describe themselves as secondhand music importers and exporters. Their showroom is at Faraday House, 8–10 Charing Cross Road, London, W.C.2, and their lists are full and varied. They will repay careful scrutiny.

Alfred A. Kalmus Ltd, of 24 Gt Pulteney Street, London, W.1

issues printed catalogues from time to time as do United Music Publishers Ltd, of 1 Montague Street, Russell Square, London, W.C.1, and duplicated lists can be had from Banks and Son (Music) Ltd, of Stonegate, York.

Other second-hand dealers include William Reeves, 1a Norbury Crescent, London, S.W.16; Leonard Hyman, 6 Eastholm, London, N.W.11; H. Baron, 50 Christchurch Avenue, London, N.W.6; W. Heffer and Sons Ltd, 3 and 4 Petty Cury, Cambridge; Basil Blackwell Ltd, 48–51 Broad Street, Oxford; A. Rosenthal Ltd, 5 Turl Street, Oxford, who issue voluminous and scholarly catalogues; and Mellor and Balley, Brynteg, Anglesey.

The music library, if carefully selected, does not get out of date. Most of the items once added, will remain and only a minor proportion will need to be discarded in any one year. So on the average, the service value of music is high. The cost of a single volume plus the cost of binding, will be comparatively high too. A score of *Billy Budd* will cost 40s bound; a complete edition of Chopin's works 81s. This should not matter. It is one of the primary justifications of a library that it makes available the things a man cannot obtain for himself, or from other sources. The proportion of new publications annually will be small; the collection will grow chiefly by the addition of more and more of the older and standard works.

There is much to be said in favour of the pooling of local resources. Libraries in a contiguous or natural geographic area could surely work out a simple system of interchange. Similarly, the public library could easily be the centre for the depositing of music used by local societies and church choirs. In this way, many compositions which normally lie idle, could be put to greater, more frequent use and so benefit the community at large.

The librarian must be on his guard against secondhand material offered as donations. It is always worth viewing but unless it is in good condition, it is not worth acquiring and he should never be hesitant in refusing in such circumstances. And it should always be accepted unconditionally. The songs of the Victorian and Edwardian ages, for example, by composers now considered of very minor importance but of some decided status in their day, would be an encumbrance.

As in all lending departments of the library, the stock must be active. Only the large music libraries can attempt comprehensiveness and even they, today, would assuredly jib at Macfarren's *Lady of the Lake*, J. F. Barnett's *Ancient Mariner* or Coleridge Taylor's *Kubla Khan*. On the other hand, sets of anthems, part songs and cantatas may be offered to even the smallest library, probably due to the dissolving of local music societies. I take the view that such items should be offered to the larger libraries, such as the Central Music Library and the Henry Watson Library. They can always be borrowed by the original recipient, in the unlikely event of their being required.

In some libraries, special tickets are issued to readers for the loan of music. These are additional to a reader's normal quota and whilst their number should not be unlimited, wide discretionary powers are required. A conductor of a string orchestra will require all the various instrumental parts plus a conductor's score. A choral society may require upwards of a score of copies of an oratorio. A pianist studying for a diploma may need all six of the Brandenburg Concertos simultaneously and if these happen to be unbound, that is, six separate compositions, the system must be geared to meet his requirements. If photocharging or bookamatic systems are used, the issuing of tickets does not arise.

The period of loan must also be flexible. It is no use expecting the choral society just mentioned to return its copies within the traditional fortnight or the increasingly popular four weeks. Three months might well be the optimum. The chamber orchestra might suffice with a month, the pianist maybe even less. On the other hand, they may each request a longer period of time for justifiable reasons and should be allowed the same latitude, without any stupid regulations interfering by way of fines, charges and renewals.

4

Binding: Storage: Display

RAPID advances have been made in binding techniques during the past twenty years. Strong cold adhesives have caused sewing processes to be abandoned, variegated coloured cloths have given variety and colour so much needed in rebindings; synthetic materials have resulted in experimentation, with pleasing results in some cases. Especially is the latter applicable to sheet music.

As a general rule, music should be purchased in its paper covers and then bound for library usage. Heavy, cumbersome volumes are to be avoided, for they are an embarrassment to user and librarian alike. It is also true that the more there is in each volume, the fewer people can use it at once. Wherever possible, therefore, music should be bound in cloth with clear lettering on the spine, running from bottom to top. It would be a great convenience if there could be consistency in spinal lettering, a matter which has been the subject of constant argument for many a long year. Volumes of music standing upright on shelves, lettered variously on the spines, cause cranium contortions and because of their comparative narrowness, their nuisance value is infinitely greater than that caused by books. Common practice is to letter from bottom to top and uniformity should be aimed at, giving class number, composer, title and score. British Standard 1544: 1949 concerning bound account and manuscript books expresses preference for spinal lettering proceeding this way.

It is the practice in some libraries to follow a colour code for different classes of music. For example, all piano music blue, organ music red, operas green and so on. This is done in the Dewsbury (Yorkshire) and Bristol libraries which doubtless helps with shelf arrangement but leads to some monotony.

Very often, volumes have to be made up, usually as a result of donations. In such cases, it is best to try to keep the works of one

composer together. Each volume so made should be paged consecu-
tively, a list of contents typed and bound in, and a title allocated
to it. Analytical cataloguing would follow. Piano duets, that is,
music for two pianos, and chamber music pose special problems.
Beethoven's String Quartets, for example, or an arrangement of
Poet and Peasant for eight hands on two pianos. The former's String
Quartets in the Peters edition happen to consist of three publishers'
volumes, Op. 18, Nos. 1–6 in Volume I; Op. 59, Nos. 1–3, Op. 74
and Op. 95 in Volume II; and Op. 130–133 and Op. 135 in
Volume III. Each string part of each volume can be bound in limp
cloth and the parts in each volume inserted in a case with envelopes
inside front cover and back boards. This makes quite a handy
volume.

The best method for the piano duet is to bind one part in such a
way that a pocket is provided in the inside back board to take the
other part which will be bound in limp cloth. These are lettered on
the front cover, a note is made on the label or inside front cover of
the accompanying part, which is checked at each time of issue and
return. Of course, there is nothing to prevent the binding of the two
parts in separate volumes, but as they are usually used together, the
former method is to be preferred. Orchestral parts and sets of vocal
music are even more troublesome. The former are best sewn separately into manila covers and the whole kept either in a pamphlet
box, in a case made to measure, or in a portfolio. Each part is
lettered with the title of the work and instrument, and a check list
affixed to the container giving the number of parts. The traditional
nomenclature for full scores can be followed: pic. fl. ob. cor.ang. cl.
bn. sax. corni. tr. tromb. tuba. timp. tamb. D. cym. harp. glock.
xyl. v.I. v.II. vla. vlo. d.bass. pf.

Vocal sets are best kept in boxes or portfolios, preferably each
copy sewn into manilla covers to afford protection and prolong its
life. These can soon deteriorate if not treated properly in the first
place. Titling of each copy should be done and the voice quoted.
The brown paper parcels so often seen, are no credit to librarianship, not even if tied with legal tape!

Sheet music need not be the perplexing problem it was. To bind
each copy separately is the real and tidiest solution. There are a
variety of methods. First is to sew or staple sheet music into stout
manila covers which are then lettered along the front cover, parallel
with the spine. They can be filed in drawers or in a vertical file.

A second method is to use the binder's cut flush style, that is, the preservation of the original title by pasting it to a thin board and strengthening the joints. The cover can be laminated for protection. A third way is to have a limp binding, the music being sewn into strong endpapers which are then pasted on to the cloth covers. A fourth method, which as far as I can adjudge, is the most successful and certainly the most contemporary, is to have the copy encased in a cover with a clear plastic front. This plastic is not titled, but as the cover title of the music is preserved, titling is unnecessary. Above all, the music should open flat and stay so.

The shelving of music needs care. Short spans and deep shelves are the answer for bound scores. Shelves should be 12 inches wide and partitions provided at no more than 12-inch spaces. The distance between shelves vertically must be a minimum of 15 inches. I prefer to shelve music standing upright on its bottom edges, but there is the possibility of its shelving lying down as it were, that is, on the back boards. Certainly this makes the reading of the spinal lettering easier, or it should do, if a consistent pattern of lettering has been followed.

As I said previously, sheet music can be adequately housed in vertical filing cabinets, or in drawers specially made for the purpose, as in the illustrations of the music department of the Malmö Central Library in Sweden (pp. 80–81). Here the arrangement and storage of music has been carefully considered and the whole appearance is one of smartness and compactness, with clever line drawings introduced into the guides to the contents of individual drawers. Box files can be used for unbound copies of sheet music and for sets of music although frequent handling by the public wrecks the order.

Miniature scores require special shelving. They will fit comfortably on to shelves $7\frac{1}{2}$ inches wide, again with 12-inch centres or less, and with $9\frac{1}{2}$ inches between shelves. Unfortunately the otherwise elegant Penguin scores were issued in an oblong style and they upset normal shelving calculations. Shallow drawers for vertical filing are a decided possibility, for the scores soon get untidy when they are kept on open shelves. This would be non-standard equipment and would have to be specially made but little ingenuity is required to give a container which is functional and of smart appearance.

As far as display goes, peg-board screens, wire meshes and even soft board panels can all be used profitably. A little ingenuity again, an eye for design and lettering and the effect is satisfying. The music librarian who has the task of arranging and presenting gramophone recitals is much better off, for record sleeves are ideal material in making attractive, eye-catching displays. Book jackets these days are finely done; disc sleeves are even finer, being lavish in colour and invariably gay in design. Messrs. J. B. Cramer and Co. have issued a set of panels on musical instruments; *Pictorial Education* has featured Musical Instruments through the Ages; photographs of performers and concerts are easily come by; Glyndebourne programmes provide a wealth of material – and so I could go on. There is no excuse for the music department being drab and dull.

5

Classification

LIONEL MCCOLVIN in his book *Music in Public Libraries* formulated a simple classification scheme suitable for the average public library. Certain general principles guided him and they are worth repeating here.

The first is that musical scores and books on music should be clearly distinguished. For this there are two reasons. Firstly, the field of music and the field of musical literature are not quite the same; though certain main divisions and subdivisions may be the same for both, on the whole each calls for different treatment; no one could prepare a schedule for music which would be equally suitable for musical literature or vice versa. Secondly, even if one classified sequence of music and literature were possible on paper, it could not be achieved in application. Most musical scores are quarto or folio; most books on music are octavo. Thus there *must* be two sequences on the shelves. Obviously, the best course is to provide, not two unsatisfactory parallel sequences, but one sequence for all music *followed* by another sequence for all musical literature.

The second principle is that the practical purpose of the user is the most distinctive basis for the subdivision of the music. One might sub-arrange music historically and nationally, by composer, or even alphabetically by composer. Such an arrangement would suit the listener but it would not help the user who played an instrument, or desired any particular type of music, such as opera.

As there will always be an author catalogue to help the listener, the music should obviously, be classified according to the instrument, voices, and so on, employed in its performance. As a general rule, this is all the subdivision that is necessary; it is sufficient, for example, to bring together all the music for piano solo; to divide it further by form is unnecessary, confusing and often impracticable, when we consider styles of composition such as rondos, preludes, fugues, sonatas and mazurkas, to mention but a few.

One implication of this principle of classifying by instrument is that whenever a work is *arranged* for an instrument, other than that for which it was originally written, that copy should go with the instrument for which it is *arranged*. For example, piano solo versions of orchestral music go with piano solo music.

The third principle is that the sequence of the schedules should be based as far as possible upon the evolution of the art. Attempts to carry logic and historical order too far would produce an unworkable and confused scheme. Yet it seems sensible to place first the types of music that came first and to proceed from the simple to the complex, from the one to the many. So we place vocal music first and instrumental music next. The vocal music starts with solos and proceeds through that for two and more voices, to the complex combinations of voices and instruments such as opera. The instrumental music begins with that for wind instruments – wood without reed, wood with reeds, metal – followed by that for strings – without bow, with bow, with keyboard and so on.

Next are combinations of instruments, first the few (chamber music), then the many (orchestra). Within this general outline we have not indulged in theoretical niceties. For example, the organ is a wind instrument but, from a performer's point of view, it has most in common with the stringed piano.

The classification of musical literature consists of much the same sequence for that part of it which deals with the history and practice of the various types of music, vocal and instrumental. This part is, however, preceded by sections dealing with general questions and musical theory, and followed by sections for philosophy, appreciation, education, history, criticism and biography.

The following schedules are provided with a notation which will enable them to be substituted for the music (780) section of Dewey. Those who prefer to use Dewey as it stands may separate musical scores from literature by appending the letter 'M' to the former. Or they may adopt the simple method of moving the decimal point one number forward for music, in which case, for example, 78·2 = operas and 782 = books on opera.

Vocal Music

780	Solo vocal music—
	Collections: General
780·1	Collections: National music, by country, A–Z.

Or, if preferred, subdivide by country as Dewey –
·13 – ·199. Place here collections of national music even if
not entirely vocal – for example, 'songs and dances of Russia'.
This may, if desired, be used as the general place for all
collections of national music, instrumental and/or vocal.
Added catalogue entries would have to be provided.

    If subdivided ·13 – ·199 use ·11 and ·12 for racial songs
(for example, Jewish, Gipsy, etc.)

780·2	Collections: Special—
·21	Songs for children. Collections.
·22	Songs for children by individual composers, A–Z.

Only to be used if it is desired to bring all children's songs
together; otherwise prefer 780·3.

·24	Special types of songs – for example, sea-songs, shanties, hunting songs.
·26	Songs for special occasions, days, celebrations.
·27	Music hall and comic songs.
780·3	Songs by individual composers, A–Z.
780·4	Concerted vocal music.
	General collections and miscellaneous concerted vocal music by individual composers (for example, duets, quartets, bound together).
·41	Duets – mixed voices – individual composers, A–Z.
·419	– collections.
·42	– female voices – individual composers, A–Z.
·429	– collections.
·43	– male voices – individual composers, A–Z.
·439	– collections.
	Trios, quartets, quintets, sextets.
·44	– mixed voices – individual composers, A–Z.
·449	– collections.

·45	– female voices – individual composers, A–Z.
·459	– collections.
·46	– male voices – individual composers, A–Z.
·469	– collections.
	Works for chorus—
·47	– mixed voices – individual composers, A–Z.
·479	– collections.
·48	– female voices – individual composers, A–Z.
·489	– collections.
·49	– male voices – individual composers, A–Z.
·499	– collections.

Note : Prefer ·41 – ·46 for works which *may* be sung by soloists or by several singers to each part, using ·47 –·49 for definitely choral works (that is, intended for several singers to each part).

| 780·5 | Sacred music – collections. |
| ·51 | Sacred solos. |

This heading to be used chiefly for cross reference.

·52	Anthems.
·53	Services, liturgy, ritual – general, collections.
·531	Church of England.
·535	Roman Catholic.
·536–9	Other churches.
·55	Psalms.
·56	Masses, requiems, and parts thereof.
·58	Hymns – general.
·581	Church of England.
·583–6	Other churches.
·588	– temperance and revivalist songs and hymns.
·589	Carols.
·59	Religious music of non-Christian religions.
780·6	Oratorios, cantatas and non-dramatic works for soloists and chorus with or without accompaniment. A–Z by composer.
·69	Collections.

Note : Includes both sacred and secular works. The general distinction between this heading and 780·5 and 780·7 is that music going in 780·5 is normally part of a

religious service or ceremony and that going in 780·7 is
normally intended for stage presentation.

780·7	Operas, A–Z by composer.
780·79	Collections.
780·8	Musical Comedies, light operas, revues. A–Z by composer.
780·89	Collections.
780·9	Other vocal music – including miscellaneous collections not better elsewhere.

INSTRUMENTAL MUSIC – SOLO AND DUET

Note : In this class all music for piano and another
instrument goes under that other instrument (for example,
'duet for violin and piano' under violin; also 'violin solo
with piano accompaniment' goes under violin, where also
will be placed items for unaccompanied violin).

Music for two instruments neither of which is the piano is
best placed under the instrument with the higher average
compass (for example, 'violin and cello' under violin); if
both have comparable compasses place under the less
common instrument (for example, 'violin and flute' under
flute). In all such cases raise added entries.

781	Collections.
781·1	*Wind instruments—*
·11	Flute.

Note : A–Z by composers under each, with if necessary,
·119 for collections. Similarly under all appropriate headings
throughout unless specially provided for.

·112	Recorder.
·12	Oboe. Cor Anglais.
·13	Clarinet.
·14	Bassoon.
·15	Trumpet, cornet.
·16	Horn.
·17	Trombone.
·18	Saxophone.
·19	Other wind instruments, A–Z.

Including bagpipe, accordion, as well as such instruments as
tuba and harmonica.

Stringed instruments—

781·2	Harp and harp family.
·23	Non-bowed instruments – plectral.
·24	Lute
·25	Guitar.
·26	Mandolin.
·27	Banjo.
·28	Zither.
·29	Other.

Bowed instruments—

781·3	Violin solos – individual composers, A–Z.
·31	Studies: exercises.
·32	– collections.
·33	Violin duets (that is, two violins)
·34	Viola – individual composers, A–Z.
·349	– collections.
·35	Violoncello – individual composers, A–Z.
·36	– collections.
·37	Double bass.
·38	Obsolete bowed instruments, for example, viols, viola da gamba.
·39	Miscellaneous – for example, collections for various instruments, works for combinations not elsewhere provided for.

Keyboard instruments—

781·4	Piano solos – individual composers, A–Z.
781·5	Piano solos – collections.
781·6	Piano duets – one piano, four hands. Individual composers, A–Z.
·61	– collections.
·64	– two pianos.
·66	Other piano music – for example, three pianos.
781·7	Organ music – individual composers, A–Z.
781·8	Organ music – collections.
781·9	Miscellaneous instrumental music – for example, for children's instruments, for percussion, bells.

CHAMBER AND ORCHESTRAL MUSIC

782	Collections and volumes containing music for two or more combinations if not better elsewhere.

Chamber music—

782·1   Duets and Trios for strings.

This and the following classes may be subdivided – for example, '2 violins and cello,' 'violin, viola, cello,' etc. – but this is not usually necessary.

·2   Trios for piano and strings.
·3   Quartets for strings.

If desired, ·3 can be reserved for works for two violins, viola and cello, and subdivisions ·31–·39 provided for other combinations.

·4   Quartets for piano and strings.

If desired, ·4 can be reserved for works for piano, violin, viola and cello, and subdivisions ·41–·49 provided for other combinations.

·5   Quintets, sextets, septets, etc., for strings alone and for piano and strings.

May be subdivided if necessary.

·6   Chamber music for wind instruments, for wind and strings, for wind, strings and piano, etc.

May be subdivided if necessary.

Orchestral music—

782·7   Orchestral music – full scores (and parts) – individual composers, A–Z.
·76   – collections.
·8   Military band music.
·85   Brass band music.
·89   Other instrumental music, for example, dance band music.

Miscellaneous—

782·9   Miscellaneous collections of vocal and instrumental music not better elsewhere.
·99   Miniature scores.

PART TWO – MUSICAL LITERATURE

General

783   Encyclopaedias, dictionaries and general comprehensive works.

Put biographical dictionaries here rather than in 789·2.
Put encyclopaedias limited to a country here, but put those dealing with a special subject with that subject.

·01   Musical terms – terminology.
·02   Periodicals – in English, A–Z.
·03   – in foreign languages.
·031   Periodicals : indexes.
·04   Year books, almanacks, calendars.
·05   Bibliography.
·051   Thematic catalogues.
·059   Music printing, publishing.
·0595   Music libraries – methods.
·06   Societies and other organizations.

Including congresses, conferences, festivals, exhibitions. Educational organizations go in 783·07.

·07   Teaching institutions, Conservatoires, colleges.

Note : Methods of teaching and musical education go in 787·5.

·08   Miscellaneous generalia. Polygraphy, collections.

THEORY AND PRACTICE

783·1   Theory of music and general practice.

·2   Elements. Rudiments.
·3   Harmony.
·4   Counterpoint, canon and fugue.
·5   Form.
·6   – special forms, for example, sonata form, variations.
·7   Composition.
·8   Acoustics.
·9   Miscellaneous theoretical questions and general practical topics, A–Z – for example, atonality, dictation, ear-training, extemporization, handwriting, interpretation, intervals, melody, memory,

modulation, notation, ornamentation, pantonality, phrasing, rhythm, scales and modes, score-reading, temperament, tempo, temporubato, thoroughbass, time (metronome), tonality, transcription, transposition.

784	Practice of music. General.
·1	Singing. Voice culture, production.
·12	Children's voices. Class singing.
·13	Church choirs – training.
·15	Special topics – for example, diction, pronunciation of foreign languages.
·17	Interpretation of vocal music, expression.
·19	History of singing. Singers.
784·2	Song. Solo vocal music.

Including history of vocal music in general.

·3	Concerted vocal music. Part songs. Madrigals.
·4	Choral music and choral singing. Choirs. Choral societies. Oratorio and cantata. Conducting.
·6	Church music and sacred music. Oratorio. Chorales. Motets.
·7	Hymns. Congregational singing. Descants.
·75	Carols.
784·8	Operatic music. General – historical and descriptive.
·84	Staging and production.
·85	Operatic singing and technique. Acting.
·86	Libretti.
·87	Operetta. Light opera. Musical comedy.
·88	Incidental music. Music in the theatre.
784·9	Ballet, mime, and other special applications of music.
785	Instruments. Technical, historical. General. Also general works on instrumental music.
785·1	Wind instruments: Wood.
·12	Flute and flute family
·13	Piccolo
·14	Oboe
·15	Cor anglais
·16	Clarinet
·18	Bassoon
785·2	Wind instruments: brass and miscellaneous.

·22	Trumpet
·23	Cornet
·24	Horn
·25	Trombone
·26	Tuba
·27	Saxhorn family
·28	Saxophone family
·29	Other wind instruments.
785·3	Harp and harp family.
·33	Non-bowed instruments – plectral, etc.
·34	Lute.
·35	Guitar.
·36	Mandolin.
·37	Banjo.
·38	Zither.
·39	Other.
785·4	Bowed instruments. The Violin family in general.
·41	Violin (and family) – history, early forms, manu-facture.
·45	Violin playing. Technique – special topics, for example, the bow.
·47	Violinists.
·48	Violin music.

Note: This and all similar headings are, of course, for books about music.

785·5	Viola – general, history and manufacture.
·52	– playing.
·53	– music.
·54	Cello – general, history and manufacture.
·55	– playing.
·56	– music.
·58	Double bass.
·59	Other.
	Keyboard instruments.
785·6	Pianoforte.
·61	History, early forms.
·63	Manufacture, repair and tuning.
·65	Pianoforte playing. Technique.
·66	– special topics, for example, accompanying.

·67	Pianists.
·68	Pianoforte music.
·69	Piano-player, pianola.
785·7	Organ.
·71	History, early forms.
·73	Construction. Design. Organ stops.
·74	Organ playing. Technique.
·75	– special topics, for example, arranging for organ.
·76	Organists.
·77	Organ music.
·78	Harmonium. American organ.
·79	Cinema organ.
785·8	Other instruments – for example, percussion, bells.
·86	Bells. Church bells.
785·9	Mechanical instruments, reproductive and transmissive processes.
·92	Musical box, hurdy-gurdy, barrel organ. For piano-player *see* 785·69.
·93	Percussion.
·94	Gramophone and gramophone records.
·95	Tape recorders and tapes.
·95	Chinese bells.
·96	Film recording of sound. Also similar processes, for example, Blattner.
·98	Wireless and Television.
786	Chamber music.
·1	Performance, technique.
·2	Music for chamber music players. Composition, works.
·3	Orchestra and orchestral music.
·4	Orchestration. Instrumentation.
·5	Orchestral music.
·6	Conducting.
·7	Military and Brass bands.
·8	Percussion Bands.
·9	Dance band. Dance music. Jazz. Swing. Pops.

AESTHETICS, APPRECIATION, STUDY

| 787 | Appreciation. |
| ·1 | Aesthetics, philosophy and psychology. |

·2	Special topic – for example, musical genius, inspiration.
·3	Special relations – for example,
·33	– music and social life.
·36	– music and industry.
·361	– music and health.
·38	– music and literature.
·39	Musical criticism.
·4	Study and teaching of music. General.

For adult education, *see also* 787

·5	Special systems, for example, eurhythmics.
·55	Special topics, for example, the school orchestra.
·6	Teaching of young children.
·7	Teaching in secondary and public schools.
·75	Music at the universities.
·78	Teaching of special classes, for example, the blind.
·8	Musical examinations.

HISTORY, CRITICISM, BIOGRAPHY

788	History and criticism. General.
·01	Early. Ancient. Primitive.
·02	Medieval.
·04	16th century.
·05	17th century.
·06	18th century.
·07	19th century.
·08	20th century.
788·1	Special topics. May be divided by country ·03–·09.
·12	Folk music in general.
·149	National music.
·16	Programme music.
·18	Style.
	By country –
788·2	England.
·21	Early medieval.
·22	16th century.
·23	17th century.
·24	18th century.
·25	19th century.
·26	20th century.

·28	Scotland.
·285	Ireland.
·287	Wales.
·289	British Empire.
	Prefer elsewhere for individual countries.
·29	Special topics – for example, English folk music.
788·3	Germany and Austria, etc.
·4	France.
·5	Italy.
·6	Spain and Portugal.
.7	Russia.
·8	Other European countries, A–Z.
·9	Asia. General.
·91	Arabia.
·92	China.
·925	Japan.
·93	India.
·94	Other Asiatic countries, A–Z.
·95	Africa.
·96	America. North America.
·97	American negro (also negro in general).
·975	American Indian.
·976	Canada.
·977	Mexico.
·978	South America.
·98	Australasia.
·99	Non-national. Racial.
·993	Gipsy music.
·995	Jewish music and musicians. Hebrew music.
789	Biography. Individual, A–Z.
·2	Collected. General may be divided by country.
	·03–·099
·3–8	– special classes.

         For added entries. Divide as scheme.

MISCELLANEOUS

789·9	Miscellaneous matters and cross references.
·91	Concerts. Concert going.
·92	Programmes. Programme making.

·93	Music in the home.
·94	Construction, of concert halls, auditoria, opera houses.
·95	Law relating to music. Copyright, performing rights.
·96	Music, the state and local government.
·97	Literature with musical interest.
·98	Scrap books, oddments, souvenirs, autographs.
·989	Musicians' work in other fields.
·99	Musical rarities. First editions. Rare editions. Manuscripts. Facsimiles.

Note: The Subject Index to this Classification scheme is not printed separately because the entries in later sections of the book (Vols I and II) are arranged according to the scheme and, consequently, the subject index to Part II will act as a subject index to these schedules (783–789) and the subject index to the lists in Vol II will serve similarly (780–782).

THE DEWEY DECIMAL CLASSIFICATION SCHEME

The 16th edition of the *Dewey Decimal Classification Scheme*, 1958, made few significant alterations to the 14th edition. It merely underwent a cleaning-up process and Dewey's scheme, followed implicitly, makes the arrangement of music from a user's viewpoint both cumbersome, illogical, and well-nigh unworkable. Cross-classification abounds. For instance, works about the organ and its music now go at 783·1 in the section headed Sacred Music: organ music itself goes at 786·8 in the other works for keyboard instruments. Incidentally, fugues go at 786·82 with or without preludes, but preludes themselves are at 786·83. We also have such unnecessary and antediluvian headings as offertories and voluntaries which could equally well be preludes and fugues.

A note at the beginning of the 780 class recommends, as McColvin does, the use of an M before the class number to distinguish scores from books. Does any library, in fact, shelve its books and scores together? It is physically impracticable. There is a number 780·071 for musicians, with subdivisions for composers 780·071 1: interpreters and performers 780·071 2: and amateurs 780·073. Musical biography is covered by 780·92. Private patronage and official patronage are separated at 780·074 and 780·075 respectively. Music festivals receive the number 780·79 but song and choral festivals are to be placed at 784·5. It gets curiouser and curiouser! Collected works about music by one or more authors go at 780·8 with collected scores of individual composers at 780·81 and collected scores by two or more composers at 780·82.

Miniature pocket scores, as the heading reads, are to be arranged at 780·84 either alphabetically by compilers and composers, or they are to be classified with the scores of conventional size prefixing MM to the number and adding author numbers. We are given MM 785·115 4 for Beethoven's 5th Symphony, as an example. Miniature scores, of necessity, must be shelved away from the full scores and it is an impossibility to get such class marks as this on their spines. Were it possible, I cannot imagine the result as anything but a confusing mass of narrow images bespattered with long numbers and letters. After all this, is there any need to go further than a straightforward alphabetical arrangement by composer? Convincing arguments against such an arrangement for music scores generally are noticeable by their absence and I am sure this is the best possible solution in the average-sized library, which can be taken to mean a library serving up to 100,000 population. It is certainly the arrangement which the user can understand and more easily follow.

Collected editions, admittedly, would pose a problem, but the catalogue would indicate the filing symbol. For example, the Cramers Collected edition of organ compositions could be shelved under Cramer as publisher, or under Martin Shaw as editor. Such an arrangement would naturally affect the provision of subject headings in the catalogue.

On the other hand, the fullest exploitation of the collection will result from keeping instrumental music together. McColvin and Reeves favoured this type of classification in fact, but if a classified catalogue is used, the whole range of music under different media will be seen.

Let us return to Dewey however. At 780·92, 'Criticism and Appraisal of work of individual musicians', there are three notes. The first says you classify here books about musicians composing or performing in more than one medium. Drs Thalben Ball, Eric Thiman and Francis Jackson would therefore be found here. The second note says that this number may, if preferred, include musicians working in one medium. So we have, in fact, enough scope here to include every musician, be he amateur or professional. Biography, however, only goes in libraries which classify biography by subject, and an italicized note says 'for criticism and appraisal of individual musicians working in one medium, see the medium, for example of violinists 787·108 1; biography of musicians 927·8'. I talked a little earlier, of the 16th edition of Dewey being a cleaning-up process. The brushes have not reached this particular section.

781·7 is a marvellous innovation. Here are theories and forms of music from a racial or national viewpoint, formerly classified at 780·9. A note tells us that the history of music in specific countries goes at 780·93–780·99. On the other hand, the music of modern peoples and races goes at 781·74 to 781·79, divided geographically like 940–999 and the example given is German music 781·743. I suppose if the title of a book read, 'The history of music in Germany', we should put it at 780·943!

It is time I said something on the credit side, for I am not one who ranges himself against Dewey generally, and this comes from a view of 782 which has been improved. Gone are the ludicrous subdivisions of opera – grand, comic and satiric, bouffe and operettas. All now are intended to go at 782·1. The production of operas has been moved from 792·4 – 792·6 to 782·07, thus bringing like with like. Operettas, however, have been moved from 782·1 to 782·81, and we are told that musical comedies and revues go here. But comic and satiric opera are to be classified at 782·1! Despair, then, you Gilbert and Sullivan fans. Comic opera – I think so. Satiric opera – I think so again. Musical comedy – I would say it is. So what does the poor classifier do? I could think of dozens more comic operas from the 1900–1930 era.

Complete large sacred choral works, we are told, should be classified at 783·3. Hence, *Elijah*, *Messiah* and *St Matthew Passion*. The music itself (scores and parts) are to be classified at the subdivisions of 783·35. Collections of sacred oratorios by two or more composers go at 783·352; single works and collections by one composer go at 783·354. Christmas music is allocated the number 783·66. *Messiah* could therefore go here, or at least, the first part of it could! Congregational singing, that is hymnody, psalmody and hymn tunes are classified at 783·9. The music itself is put at 783·95. I can only ever remember seeing one hymn book with tunes only and no words. Even if this were general, however, there would be no justification for two separate placings.

The numbers for vocal music in 784 do not relieve the mono-
tonous recurrence of cross-classifications. Choruses and part-songs
become 784·1 and yet songs for one or more voices are placed at
784·3. Songs for unorganized groups, that is, those not organized
primarily for musical purposes, are to go at 784·6. This presumably
accommodates songs for townswomen's guilds!!

Again, too, we have many numbers allocated for the music itself –
seven in fact – with absurdities such as 784·66 which takes songs for
Rotary Clubs with 784·660 6 for the music itself. Collections of
songs for male voices can go at 784·87 or 784·106 83. Two charac-
teristics therefore are used quite extravagantly and indiscriminately,
the types of songs, that is their nature, and the number of voices for
which they are intended.

Instrumental music at 785 now includes the brass and military
band which have been moved from 788. Romantic idyllic music
785·3 could be equally well placed at 785·465, the salon orchestra
and its music and at 785·475 music for the string orchestra. The
latter number accommodates overtures, whereas independent
overtures for symphony orchestras go at 785·55. *Zampa, Poet and
Peasant, Light Cavalry* – some of the most well-known overtures are
played also by the salon orchestra, could be played by strings only,
and they are also romantic compositions. Where then, are they
classified? 785·85 takes suites for the symphony orchestra. *Peer Gynt*
therefore. Isn't this romantic, idyllic music too?

786 keyboard instruments and their music, has two main divisions,
string and wind instruments. Studies and exercises for the piano and
organ take 786·33 and 786·73 respectively. These are extended – one
cannot say subdivided – for elementary, intermediate and advanced
instruction tutors. Take the numbers 786·36–786·38 and 786·76–
786·78 respectively. Apart from the fact that these are obvious subdivisions, there is hardly any necessity for the three grades, and in
fact, the revisers of Dewey decided they were unnecessary for the
violinist, who only has one number 787·107 for his tutors!

Gramophone or phonograph records are classified with talking
books at 789·912 under the heading 'Electronic musical instruments'.
Nothing for recorded tapes in the schedules and by this time, there
must have been justification for subdivision of records by their
various speeds as well as by the method of reproduction – mono and
stereo.

All in all, the 16th edition of Dewey has only added to the

confusion which the 14th edition caused. I would say that the main differences are the numbers now to be used for musical scores themselves, which represent no real gain and have been taken to absurd limits as I have shown. After all, the responsibility for showing where an item is shelved rests with the cataloguer. I can well imagine the difficulties a cataloguer would experience in giving subject entries to music if the Dewey notation were closely followed. Suppose we had, in fact, a bound volume of oratorios. The classification number would be 783·352 – collections by two or more composers. The subject entry could only be oratorios: collections. This would convey little to the consultant of the catalogue and it is a heading I should resist using and rely on the analytical entries.

Take also children's songs. If they are solo songs, they are classified at 784·306 11: if on the other hand they are choruses, madrigals, glees, rounds or catches, they go at 784·106 81: should they be songs for the home, they take 784·610 6: or school songs, 784·62; 784·622 for colleges and university, 784·623 06 for secondary schools and 784·624 06 for elementary schools. Should they be national in character, then 784·71 would be appropriate. Imagine the ludicrous headings these numbers could produce:

SONGS, children's: solos	784·306 11
SONGS, children's: for use in the home	784·610 6
or SONGS, children's: domestic	,,
or SONGS, children's: fireside	,,
SONGS, children's: school – elementary	784·624 06
SONGS, children's: choruses	784·106 81

I just cannot imagine any useful purpose being served by so many classification numbers, nor can I think of volumes of music which would fit these various numbers, were they desirable. And the much-loved nursery rhymes and their music, where to put them? 784·624 06 – Elementary School songs: or 372·215 Songs and games in the kindergarten and nursery school?

BRITISH CATALOGUE OF MUSIC

The *British Catalogue of Music* already mentioned, compiled by E. J. Coates, uses a faceted scheme of classification and is therefore capable of representing each characteristic of any musical composition. For example, a selection from *South Pacific* arranged for accordion solo has the symbol RSPMK/CM/JR. This can be broken down as follows:

R　　　　organ
RS　　　　accordion
RSPM　　unaccompanied accordion solos
RSPMK　　arrangements
RSPMK/CM　　from musical plays
RSPMK/CM/JR　　film music

A pretty formidable notation, especially when one is accustomed to the numerical. Mnemonic features we so easily recognize in Dewey, are present in the B.C.O.M. on a much lesser scale and more unrecognizable too, but for a large music collection, where minute classification illustrating various aspects is called for, this scheme has everything in its favour.

Let us look at the classification in a little more detail. The obvious, significant division is that of musical literature, and music scores and parts. The former takes the letters A and B: the latter, the letters C to Z, excluding I and O in order to avoid confusion, as I have already said.

A covers general works, with common subdivisions. The following selection for example, will serve to illustrate the general layout:

	A(B)	Musical periodicals
Forms	A(C)	,,　　encyclopedias
	A(D)	,,　　essays
	A(E)	,,　　anecdotes: personal reminiscences

	A(M)	Persons in music
	A(MM)	Musical profession
	A(MN)	Music as a career
	A(P)	Musical individuals
Subjects	A(V)	Study of music, musical education
	A(W)	Concerts
	A(X)	History of music
	A(Y)	Music of particular localities
	A(Z)	Music in relation to other subjects

The common form subdivisions appear in round brackets and there are nine of them.

Further subdivision takes place by form when the oblique stroke is used:

A/AM	Theory of music
A/CY	Technique of music
A/D	Composition
A/E	Performance
A/F	Recording

Whilst the three latter subjects are each musical techniques, they are not subdivisions of A/CY as might be expected and as would be the case in an hierarchical scheme of classification. To go on a little further:

A/FY	Musical character
A/G	Folk music
A/H	Dance music
A/HM	Ballet music
A/JR	Film music
A/LZ	Elements of music
A/R	Harmony
A/S	Forms of music
A/Y	Fugue

AB represents works on vocal music: AC works on opera: and AD–AX works for various media which take the classification and symbols D–X, and what an exhaustive list of dance forms appears at ALH! B is used for works on individual composers. There is a certain amount of overlapping here, for A(M) is used for persons in music and A(P) individuals, whilst A(E) takes personal reminiscences. Sir Compton Mackenzie's *My Record of Music* might well be accommodated in the three A's mentioned, therefore, whilst Hesketh Pearson's *Gilbert and Sullivan* could be treated likewise, or placed at BSW, the symbol for Sir Arthur Sullivan. Sir William Schwenck Gilbert has no specific place here – legitimately so, as he was no musician – and he would therefore be classified at ACL, opera-comique. At B however, 155 composers are specifically mentioned. There are some omissions: Alan Richardson, Percy Grainger, Sir Walford Davies, Thomas Pitfield and Eric Thiman to mention but a few. Curious spellings have also been adopted for the Russian composers. For instance, Chaikovsky, Musorgsky, Prokof'ev, Rakhmaninov and Skryabin.

BZ has extensive coverage of the non-European countries which bear no relation to the ethnic/locality subdivisions listed in Auxiliary Table 6, so that any expected geographical mnemonic feature is not fulfilled. BZC is Turkey; BZD – Syria; BZEH – Afghanistan; and BZJP – Japan. In the auxiliary table, Turkey is VB; Syria VC; Afghanistan is not mentioned and Japan is VU.

Then come the actual schedules for the music itself:

C	Collections
CB–K	Vocal music
L–N	Instrumental music
P–Y	Individual instruments

These are followed by the Auxiliary Tables. Table 1 gives headings for extended subdivision under instruments and instrumental groups, PW–Y in the schedule. Table 2 is for sub-arrangement under the piano, Q, and the harpsichord QR, and gives a few additional ones which may be applied to these instruments in addition to the headings of Table 1. Similarly, Table 3 adds two headings to those in Table 1 for the organ and Table 4 adds a few headings applicable to the schedules AL–AY. Table 5 provides for Christian denominations whilst Table 6 I have mentioned. Table 7 is for period division on the lines of the Library of Congress tables, but these are not used, as far as I can see, in the B.C.O.M. itself.

The guiding factor to remember in using this scheme is that classification symbols are built up in reverse schedule order, that is by (1) executant, (2) form of composition, and (3) character of composition.

Therefore, a 'Burgundian carol arranged for female voices with recorder, trumpet and drum accompaniment' would be placed at FE/NYHDP/LF. Breaking this down into its component parts, it is:

	F	Female voices
Executant	FE	Female voices with other than keyboard accompaniment
	NYH	Wind and percussion
Form	DP	Carols
Character	LF	Christmas

The LF is taken from the Musical Character part of the Schedules, A/FY–A/LUYK and as the A is constant, it can be dropped.

To quote another example, 'The Oxford book of carols for schools arranged for recorder' becomes VSK/DP/LF/AY :

Executant – recorder – $\begin{cases} VS \\ K \end{cases}$ arrangements from auxiliary table 1

Form   DP   carols

Character $\begin{cases} LF \\ AY \end{cases}$ Christmas
                                        collections

And a third example, quite different, showing the use of auxiliary table 7, 'Easy graded old English masters; selected and edited by James Ching'. They cover the period 1563–1778. QP/AYD(XDYC216) :

Executant   Q   Piano
Form   P   Piano solo

Character $\begin{cases} AY \\ D \\ X \\ D \\ YC \\ 216 \end{cases}$ Collections
                English
                Introducing chronological subdivision
                1500 AD
                63
                A subtraction to give the total of years covered

6

Cataloguing

It is not easy to catalogue music satisfactorily. For this, there are two main reasons. First, music is universal and knows no language bounds. A work can be published in many editions each in a different language; yet it is the same thing so far as the musician is concerned. Admittedly, a vocalist might want Schumann's Lieder with German words especially; a Mozart opera may be of no use to him unless the words are in English. But the music itself is the same whether it be played by a Finn, an Italian or a Brazilian. To make matters worse, composers themselves use confusing mixtures of languages for the titles and descriptions of their works and to cite Mozart again, he used German and Italian libretti for his operas, for example, Le Nozze de Figaro: Die Hochzeit des Figaro; Die Zauberflöte: Il flauto magico.

Second, the musical unit is not as fixed and indivisible as, say, the literary unit. Extracts from, and parts of, a larger work are frequently issued, sometimes with individual titles without any direction to the parent work. Whole works and parts alike are arranged and transcribed for all kinds of voices and instruments, other than those for which they were originally written. The cataloguer must therefore:

(1) bring together all forms, parts and editions of the same work;
(2) be able to locate a work by its title if this is distinctive;
(3) be able to find works in any form, for example, operas, oratorios, piano duets and string trios;
(4) be able to locate works for particular instruments.

I favour a classified catalogue which will arrange by form or by instrument or both and yet, by its indexes, will be able to satisfy the requirements already stated.

The following entries should be provided:

(1) Composer entries – equivalent to author entries.

(2) Subject entries which may be two-fold, according to form and/or instrument. More will be said about these later.

Additional entries may be necessary under the categories following:

(3) For author of words, that is poet or librettist. Only in special cases are these necessary. For example, when the author of the words is a person of literary importance, it may occasionally be useful to be able to gather together various settings of words, for example, Sir Alan P. Herbert, Oscar Hammerstein and Alan Melville. Such entries are, however, by way of a luxury and it is difficult to lay down any rule as to which authors should be so recorded. Similarly with libretti or in the case of dramatists whose works are adapted. Only occasionally is the work justified (for example, operatic adaptations of Shakespeare's plays or libretti by people known for other reasons, such as Arnold Bennett and E. M. Forster.)

(4) For editors, arrangers, transcribers. Entries for editors are, of course, necessary in the case of collections and other works which may be known or asked for by the editor's name. Otherwise, although the information may be given in the main entries, they are unnecessary. So are entries for arrangers, fingerers and revisers. Transcribers are in a different category. The difference between an 'arranger' and a 'transcriber' is narrow but should be borne in mind. By 'arrangement' we mean the transference of a work from the instrument or voice for which it was originally written to another instrument or voice, without the addition of any fresh musical material except maybe, an accompaniment or connecting material. For example, a song may be arranged as an instrumental solo, an orchestral work as a pianoforte solo, but in these cases there could be no doubt as to the authorship of the resulting piece. Some composers have specialized in the art of arrangement, however, and none more so than Dr Eric H. Thiman, who is well known in choral circles for his adventurous harmonies, of hymn tunes and of well-known airs. I think particularly of melodies like *Who would true valour see* and *The Daffodils*, a fascinating arrangement. There is a tendency to dismiss such settings as ordinary, involving as they do, a new approach to the accompaniment as well as to the melody, but anyone with a genuine musical ear realizes the craftsmanship and talent behind them.

A transcription implies some amount of original work on the part of the transcriber. If little, undoubtedly the main entry should be under the original composer. Should the amount of originality be great however, the form of entry is not so certain. For example, Godowsky's famous transcriptions are so far removed from the original Chopin, that they could be considered as Godowsky's compositions with the main entry under his name, and an added entry under Chopin. This is a unique example. Today, transcriptions and arrangements are synonymous.

(5) There are some works which are based upon musical material by other composers – for example, Variations on a theme. The joint code rule says enter under the composer of the variations with a cross reference from the composer of the original material. Brahms' *Variations on a theme of Haydn* would therefore go under Brahms with an added entry under Haydn. This particular work, Op. 56a, the *St Antoni Chorale*, would also have a title entry under *St Antoni Chorale*. Similarly, Sir Ralph Vaughan Williams' *Variations on a theme of Thomas Tallis*, would receive the same treatment. Would inquirers look under Haydn and Tallis in these cases? I very much doubt it, but if it is desired to play for absolute safety, then added entries would be given under their names. It is better to err on the lenient side than to fail by being too rigid.

(6) For titles. There is a tendency to over-do title entries. I think that as far as music goes, it is not often that the composer's name is unknown to the inquirer. Title entries are therefore not wanted when the title is just the name of some musical form. Twenty sonatas; Preludes and Fugues; English suites and the like. Entries under titles may be given for works with descriptive or fanciful titles if there is any likelihood of their being useful, for example, an entry under *La Paloma* would be helpful but one under the *Waldstein Sonata* would seem unnecessary. On the other hand, not everyone would recognize this as a Beethoven sonata and fewer would know the opus number, and I think it is wiser to make a title entry here also. In libraries staffed by musical personnel, it could well be superfluous but most of our collections, in public libraries at any rate, are manœuvred by non-musical personnel which makes the coverage of every contingency advisable. I would make entries for *Moonlight sonata*, the *Jupiter symphony* and the like in order to be doubly sure. Title entries for operas, light operas and musical comedies are necessary. Title entries for songs are desirable and whilst Sears' *Song Index* is a handy reference tool, the catalogue should be self-

supporting. Collections of songs, whether issued by the publishers, for example, J. B. Cramer and Co., or made up by the library itself, need analytical entries to enable the fullest exploitation of the stock both under composers and titles. The smaller the library, the greater the need.

(7) For forms, by which are meant such groupings as those of operas, cantatas, symphonies and concertos. Entries under these headings may seem superfluous as the classified catalogue will bring together many of these forms. Nevertheless, index entries will be needed to direct users to the shelf placings if nothing else.

(8) Alternative headings. These are really cross references, although in the case of titles (but not composers), it may save users' time to give actual entries. Obviously, there must be references from the various forms of a composer's name, especially with Russian composers. For example, from Strawinsky to Stravinski, but not from Stravinskii to Stravinsky. There must also be references from various forms and languages of title whenever title entries are considered necessary at all. In addition, full alternative title references are necessary under the author headings in author or classified catalogues.

(9) For joint composers, the usual cataloguing practice is followed.

Attention must be drawn at this juncture to the *Code International de Catalogage de la Musique* to be issued by the International Association of Music Libraries in five volumes. So far, the first two volumes only have been issued. Volume 1 by Franz Grasberger is *The Author Catalogue of Published Music* and was published by C. F. Peters in 1957. Volume 2 is *The Limited Code* compiled by Yvette Fedoroff and was published by Peters in 1961. Both volumes have been translated by Virginia Cunningham. Volumes 3 to 5 are announced as : 3 – *Code for full cataloguing;* 4 – *Code de catalogage des manuscrits;* 5 – *Code de catalogage des enregistrements sonores.*

The Association has surveyed the cataloguing practice and textbook material of the present century and has now formulated its international code. The President of the International Association of Music Libraries, A. Hyatt King, in his foreword, hopes the new code will suggest to older libraries, ways in which they might modify their theory and practice towards some measure of uniformity which would make easier the consultation of their catalogues by those unfamiliar with their principles. For new libraries, and for

3*

those with small but growing collections of music, the I.A.M.L. code should provide a sound starting point.

In the first chapter of Volume 1, a truism so obvious as to be overlooked, is stated. It is the nature and characteristic of music that it comes alive as an art only in the hearing. The realm of the music library includes the preservation of musical works, research into the origin and the nature of the music, and consideration of the problems of performance. Therefore, the problems of cataloguing embrace music literature, librettos, programme notes, published music and manuscripts, records and magnetic tape recordings, pictorial reproductions, photocopies and microfilms.

The basic principles of author cataloguing are followed when dealing with music, but additional factors are differences in titles, changes of key and instrumentation, number of editions, and difficulties in trying to establish the date of publication.

According to Volume 1 of the Code, the main entry consists of the following parts:

Heading
    Opus number or other numerical designation
    Title
    Work (parts of work)
    Language of the text
    Beginning of the text – [a doubtful insertion in my view]
    Class
    Key
    Instrumentation
    Edition
    Contents

Bibliographical data
    Place of publication
    Publisher
    Year
    Edition
    Plate or publication number
    Size
    Format
    Number of volumes
    Series

Notes
    Preface

Introduction
Epilogue
Dedication
Facsimile edition
With facsimile
Illustrations
Method of printing

It is interesting that, in thirteen large American libraries surveyed, there is a great degree of uniformity of practice. All of them give the publisher, the date, the main paging and the series, whilst all but one give the place of publication.

THE MAIN ENTRY

(1) The Heading.

This is generally the composer's name.

(*a*) The simplest method is to follow the form of spelling given in Grove's *Dictionary of Music and Musicians* and for composers not mentioned there, to resort to the *British Catalogue of Music*. 'See' references are to be used from variant forms where there are obvious differences.

> Tschaikovsky
> Tchaikovsky

When two or more composers are involved, the joint author rule (A.A. Code 2) can be followed.

(*b*) A Collection of works by various composers would be entered under the editor or editors when the collection has obviously been assembled by one or more persons.

> 780·4   Holst, Imogen, *editor.*
> Singing for pleasure: a collection of songs; edited for female voices by Imogen Holst. O.U.P.

(*c*) Anonymous works and works known only by their titles are entered under their titles.

> 781·9   *Fitzwilliam Virginal Book*; twenty-four pieces from the *Fitzwilliam Virginal Book*; transcribed and edited by Thurston Dart. Stainer and Bell

(*d*) Works of a corporate body should be entered under the name of the body be it a society, college, church, ministry, association or institution.

> 781·5   The Associated Board of the Royal Schools of Music.
> Pianoforte examinations 1960: grades 1 to 7

Should the body corporate be responsible for the work of one or more composers, added entries would be made under the composers' names.

(e) Cadenzas are entered under their composers with added entries under the composers of the original works. If a musician is in need of a particular cadenza, he is likely to look under the composer of the cadenza. In any event, an added entry under the composer of the original work provides for the alternative possibility of looking under his name.

> Barrère, Georges, 1876–1944.
> Cadenzas for the flute concerto in G major (K313), by Wolfgang Amadeus Mozart

(f) Librettos only, are catalogued under the author of the libretto and the entry carries the word *libretto* in order to distinguish the work from the actual score. An added entry is made under the name of the composer, however, if the Anglo-American Code rule is followed. This is wise for as an example, we know full well that Sir Edward German composed the music of *Merrie England* but we may not easily remember that the words were written by Basil Hood. An added entry under the composer provides a double safeguard.

> Hood, Basil
> *Merrie England* composed by Sir Edward German. Chappell.
> *Libretto*

(2) The Title.

Here difficulties do arise and musical knowledge becomes a real boon. The title may appear in two or more languages, and these may pose lingual problems. The key may be variously stated. Take a simple example. Here is the title-page of the Eulenberg edition of the *Eroica*:

> Symphony No. 3
> E flat major
> (*Eroica*)

by
Ludwig van Beethoven
Op. 55
Composed in 1803; completed early in 1804
First performed
7th April 1805, at Vienna, Theater an der Wien
under the direction of Beethoven.
Edited from the autograph MS by
Max Unger
Foreword by Wilh. Altmann

Ernst Eulenberg, Ltd., London, W.1
Edition Eulenberg, G.m.b.H., Zürich
Edition Eulenberg, K. – G. Stuttgart
Eulenberg Miniature Scores, New York

The cover gives, in addition, the series number of the score, 405, and gives the keys as E flat major – Mi♭ majeure – Es dur, but omits all the other detail. The main title is therefore best to follow.

(a) The obvious title is Symphony No. 3 in E flat major, Op. 55 (*Eroica*), followed by the remaining descriptions and this serves to illustrate the rule that if the title is indicative of form, type, number or key, give it in English. An added entry under Eroica in this particular case would not be amiss, despite the fact that it seems too obvious. We take too much for granted both from the public angle and from that of our own staffs.

(b) If a title is in a language other than English, the title proper is translated into English followed by the foreign form. Hector Berlioz's *Childhood of Christ*, a sacred trilogy, might be given as such, or it may be *L'enfance du Christ*, trilogie sacrée, or even *Das Heilands Kindheit*, geistliche trilogie. In an English library, the title in English is obviously to be preferred and comes first each time, in order to achieve consistency.

(c) When the item is part of a larger work, or a collection which is normally published together, it is entered under the title of the whole work or collection. This enables the complete work and selections from it to be kept together.

780·6   Handel, George Frederick, 1685–1759
         [Oratorios] *Judas Maccabeus*. Novello. *Vocal score*

Followed by:

780·42   Handel, George Frederick, 1685–1759

[Oratorios] *Judas Maccabeus (O lovely peace*: vocal duet)

Added entries would, of course, be provided:

Judas Maccabeus, by G. F. Handel. *Vocal score*. 780·6

O lovely peace (Judas Maccabeus) by G. F. Handel. *Vocal duet* 780·42

(3) The *opus number* is given when ascertainable, especially in the case of works which have no descriptive or nominative title. An *opus number* is one given to a composition in the order of its composition or publication and is an unmistakable identification, since no two works will bear the same number (excepting when the *opus* consists of two or more items published together, when they are referred to as, for example, Sonata Op. 49, No. 1 and Sonata Op. 49, No. 2). Moreover, the *opus number* system is international. The opus number may often usefully be preceded by the number in that particular form, for example, Symphony No. 3, Op. 75. A title-page which may read *Third Symphony* must be altered to the form given, as otherwise, editions of the same work would be separated in alphabetization. The number in the form should not be put *after* the opus number. This would cause confusion if an opus number comprised two or more items. For example, Beethoven's second work consists of three piano sonatas, Op. 2, No. 1; Op. 2, No. 2; Op. 2, No. 3. His second sonata for piano might be described as Sonata for pianoforte No. 2, Op. 2, No. 2. Had Beethoven published an earlier piano sonata as his first opus, his second sonata would become No. 2, Op. 2, No. 1, if this opus included other items.

Care must be taken in the case of composers whose works have been variously numbered by different editors and publishers. I think particularly of Bach, Haydn and Mozart. The Bach Gesellschaft numbering of his cantatas and chorales is as published in the Breitköpf and Härtel complete edition of 1850–1900 and has nothing to do with the order of composition or publication in previous editions. It is an arbitrary order so that a cantata with an early number can be one of his late works.

Haydn's symphonies vary between the collected edition and the Haydn Society Collection edition, which embodies more recent discoveries. For example, Symphony No. 40 in F major in the collected edition was placed as such by Mandyezewski who believed it to have been written about 1770. Later, the autograph score revealed the date of composition as 1763, thus the Haydn Society gave it the number 13a.

Mozart's works were the subject of a thematic index by Ludwig Köchel in 1862 entitled *Chronologisch-thematisches Verzeichniss sämtlicher Tonwerke Wolfgang Amade Mozarts*. 3 Aufl. This was revised by Alfred Einstein in 1937 and his arrangement is reputably more accurate chronologically. Therefore we expect an identification by Köchel number in the case of Mozart rather than an opus number.

After the number and opus number, give the key. If the work has a name, whether given by the composer or by custom, add in brackets if desired. Sometimes this may be the only distinguishing factor. The *Moonlight Sonata* is a case in point, as is the *Emperor Concerto*. There are dozens of others. As with the adjectival form already mentioned, that is, Third Symphony instead of Symphony No. 3, a title smacking of high-falutin' patronage must be reduced to its acceptable form. Beethoven's *Grand sonata for piano* is useless and absurd. Expressed in the form, Sonata for pianoforte in C major, No. 21, Op. 53 (*Waldstein*) it is unmistakable.

This leads me to a momentary digression about the conventional title. This is used to identify and to bring together all editions and arrangements of a composition. Failing its use, a concerto could also be called Konzert für piano; Piano concerto; Solo du concerto de pianoforte. Conventional titles fall into two categories, non-distinctive and distinctive. The former consist of a word indicating a class or type of musical composition which has cognates in various languages. For example, a cognate word accompanied by a cardinal or ordinal number as in *Ten canons, Missa quinta, Deuxième symphonie*, or by an adjective as we have just seen, as *Grand, Celebrated, Well-known* and *Favourite*. Distinctive conventional titles are all others, including those made up of class words or phrases modified by descriptive adjectives or adjectival phrases as in *Missa brevis, Sonate en due* and titles consisting of class words or phrases for which there are no English cognates, as *Gesange, Lieder, Morceaux*, or for which there are no English plurals, as *Canzone, Ricercare*.

Collected editions, that is, complete collections and partial collections of works in different forms and for different media of performance. These must be given a conventional or all-embracing title; for example,

Bach, Johann Sebastian 1685–1750
 [Complete works] Bach-Gesellschaft . . .
 – [Complete works] Neue Ausgabe sämtlicher Werke . . .

Collected editions can also be complete or partial in one musical form and for one medium of performance, for example:

Haydn, Franz Joseph 1732–1809
 [Piano works] Eight selected piano sonatas . . .
 – [Piano works] Twenty piano sonatas . . .

The form or nature of the work is stated unless it is implied or stated in the title:

The Marriage of Figaro: opera in four acts
Jesu Joy of Man's Desiring: chorale prelude arranged for organ
The Wasps: Aristophanic suite for symphony orchestra

State the instruments or combination, or voices for which the actual copy being catalogued is written.

(*a*) In a work for several instruments, state whether the copy is a score, that is, with parts printed above each other, page by page, or a set of parts for various instruments. If a score, state whether it is a full score, or a miniature score.

(*b*) In the case of chamber music and music for an ensemble, state the exact combination employed, except that a string quartet is assumed to be for two violins, viola and 'cello, and a piano trio is for piano, violin and 'cello unless otherwise specified.

Schubert, Franz 1797–1828
 [Instrumental works] Minuet and Finale in F major for wind octet
 For flute, oboe, 2 clarinets, 2 bassoons, 2 horns

This could be reduced to fl. ob. cl. b. corni.

(*c*) Pianoforte music may be for solo pianoforte; for piano duet, that is, one piano four hands; for two pianos four hands; or for two pianos eight hands.

(*d*) If voice parts are given, it is a vocal score. If arranged for piano and there are no voice parts, it is a piano score.

(*e*) Piano concertos may be arranged for one player, or the orchestral part may be a separate part for a second player. The form of presentation should be made clear on the catalogue entry.

(*f*) If a work is an arrangement, state that it is an arrangement and give particulars of the original work.

British Museum: working area in main music room

British Museum: The Royal Music Library

Amerika Gedenkbibliothek, Berlin

Amerika Gedenkbibliothek, Berlin

Brighton Public Libraries: Albert Spencer collection of
musical instruments

Malmö, Sweden: Music Library

Malmö, Sweden : Music Library

Styles of music bindings

(*g*) In the case of a choral work, the voices used should be stated unless it is for the normal four ranges, soprano, alto, tenor and bass, expressed s.a.t.b. Any soloists employed should be mentioned and their voices.

Vocal works. State the language or languages of the words and in the case of songs, give the range of voice for which they are intended which may be high, medium or low. Well-known arias and folk songs have been transposed into various keys and arranged in various ways from time to time. For the Associated Board's examinations, the particular transposition required is always stated.

Accompaniments. When a work is accompanied, the name of the accompanying instrument is given unless it is the piano. If a work is without accompaniment, that fact should be given.

Other particulars such as editor, arranger, transcriber, should be given but great discretion should be used. Much superfluous detail can be spread over catalogue entries and in card catalogues, the typing area is restricted. On the other hand, the Eric Thiman or Gordon Jacob arrangements of folk songs are far too good and individual to be omitted.

Imprint. This consists of the place of publication, the publisher or printer and the date. If there are many places and publishers, the first are sufficient. Most music however, is undated. When the date is readily ascertainable, it is a very useful piece of information. The abbreviation *n.d.* should be avoided. If a date is not given and it cannot be found, then no date can appear on an entry. It is ludicrous to put *n.d.* If the copyright date is the only one ascertainable, precede the date with the letter c.

Collation. This consists of the number of volumes, pages, illustrations, plates, portraits and facsimiles, the size, series and plate number. Except for first editions and rarities, most of this information is superfluous. The number of volumes should be stated if the work or works are in more than a single volume. Normally, pagination is unnecessary, but a score may be accompanied by one or more separate parts, and these should be specified. The type of score should also be stated, as full score, full score and orchestral parts, medium score, miniature score, vocal score, instrumental parts. The publishers' plate number is a serial number given by a publisher to his publications in consecutive order. It is to be found usually at the bottom of each page of a work.

Contents. Again in card catalogues, the setting-out of contents can involve many additional cards in the main entry. Contents need not be given for a composer's complete works for an instrument, or in a particular form, or for short and unrelated pieces which are numerous. The smaller the music collection, however, the greater the need for analysis. Therefore, Bach's *Complete organ works*; Chopin's *Nocturnes for piano*; and a miscellaneous collection such as *Famous opera tunes* arranged for piano by K. Godfrey, need no further listing. But composite volumes such as those issued by music publishers, for example, Cramer's *Celebrated Albums* for various instruments and voices, must have contents specified and analytical entries raised. It is quite possible that in the smaller libraries, the only copy of a particular composition is in a miscellaneous collected edition and the need for analysis becomes more urgent. For example, Cramer's *Album of light classical pieces* includes Handel's *Arrival of the Queen of Sheba*; Sinding's *Rustle of Spring*; Litolff's *Scherzo*; Borodin's *Nocturne* amongst others, all worthy of separate entries.

Arrangement of entries. Under a composer's name, three methods are possible:

(*a*) alphabetical by title;
(*b*) in classified order, that is, all piano music, all organ music, music for strings, vocal items;
(*c*) in chronological or opus number order.

In a classified catalogue, the form arrangement is taken care of. But in the index to this catalogue and in a dictionary catalogue, virtually synonymous as they are, an order of arrangement must be followed strictly in order to achieve consistency. Chronological or opus number order is obviously not practicable in the average library. A classified order has much to recommend it, although difficulties abound and the same work, or parts of it, can be separated. For example, *Marriage of Figaro* may be a vocal score; an orchestral arrangement only; a selection of arias for bass voice; a popular piano duet arrangement; or say merely the overture arranged for organ. I should say that the piano duettist would only be interested in his particular arrangement and would benefit from this form grouping. If this arrangement is adopted, key subject words must appear on the catalogue entries as *piano music*. On the other hand, a title arrangement, provided the foregoing rules are followed, may be the easier and most practical. It is Hobson's choice. As I have

said, this does bring different presentations of the same work together and the arrangement can be gleaned from the body of the
entries.

Medleys are entered under the composer of the medley if the material
is taken from two or more composers. If it is based on material by
one composer only, the entry is under the composer with an added
entry under the composer of the medley. One could hardly do anything different! C. B. Cochran's *Selections from Musical Plays and
Films* must go under Cochran. A medley from *My Fair Lady* would
be entered under the name of the composer, Frederick Loewe.

Folk tunes, anonymous songs are entered under their titles with added
entries under the names of the arrangers, for example:

> *Old King Cole :* traditional Folk Song; set to music for T.T.B.B. by
> Harold Noble;
> *Macdonald's Farm :* for full chorus of women's voices with piano
> accompaniment; *arr.* by David Strickler.

Subject entries. I am sure it would be conceded that a classified, that
is, a systematic arrangement of music, is to be preferred. James Duff
Brown advocated using the general heading *Music* and subdividing
this, thus bringing all music together in one place in the catalogue.
Ruth Wallace's *The Care and Treatment of Music in a Library* gives a
long list of subject headings but like Dewey's classification, it goes to
illogical lengths by dividing Piano Music into Arabesques, Ballades,
Caprices, Mazurkas, Rondos, Scherzos and so on. A reasonable
minimum of headings is preferred and the Limited Code of the
International Cataloguing Commission gives the following:

Air	Motet
Ballet	Opera
Cantata	Operetta
Chamber Music	Oratorio
Chorus	Orchestra
Comic Opera	Plainsong
Dance	Psalm
Folksong and Folkdance	Song
Manual, Tutor, Exercises	Treatise

This is allocation of headings by type of music and it would be
difficult to place sonatas, preludes and fugues under these headings.
Similarly, air, folk-song and song could easily lead to cross placings.
Presumably, symphonies, concertos, symphonic preludes and the
like would be called orchestra. The International Code rightly

suggests that additional entries be made and the example chosen is Beethoven's Sonatas for violin and piano. The possible headings here are:

(1) Piano;
(2) Sonata;
(3) Violin;
(4) Chamber Music – two instruments.

The piano sonatas could only be given the headings:

(1) Piano – 19th century; and
(2) Sonatas.

The trios would be allocated the headings:

(1) Chamber music – three instruments; and
(2) Trios.

For simplification, divisions by instruments and types only are recommended for retention, to the exclusion of form. I see no point whatever in having Piano Music subdivided by period. Imagine the number of entries which would be raised if there were unit entry cataloguing. A single entry giving the class number would suffice in a dictionary catalogue and period subdivision is unnecessary.

Admittedly, it is easy to cavil, but if these eighteen subject headings only are used, then the need for 'see' references increases, as for example, Symphony *see* Orchestra; Sonata *see* under the name of the instrument, or, if for two instruments, under Chamber music; Concerto *see* under the name of the solo instrument. It is because of these difficulties that I prefer a classified arrangement, however simple it may be, thus dispensing automatically with many problems concerned with subject headings.

7

British Public Libraries

BATTERSEA – an extensive collection of gramophone records and sponsors music lectures. Lists of recent additions of books on music and records issued and there are quarterly Music Library Notes in the *Battersea Booklist*. A Music Librarian is employed on Salary grade A.P.T.II.

BERMONDSEY – 4,242 gramophone records. Issues a mimeographed catalogue of their collection with periodical lists of records. Classification scheme – Brown. Has a variety of excellent recording equipment.

BETHNAL GREEN – 2,414 items and 1,770 records. A stencilled catalogue issued. Classification scheme – Brown. A Music Librarian is employed on salary grade A.P.T.II plus a General Division assistant.

BIRMINGHAM – 18,000 books and scores.

BOURNEMOUTH – 8,000 items, with 600 miniature and 400 full scores. The collection was originally formed by John B. M. Camm, and as musical literature is one of the subjects in which Bournemouth specializes, the collection is growing rapidly, as all new publications are purchased.

BRADFORD – plan to have a new music department in their projected modern central library which will be erected in 1966. Promote weekly lunchtime recitals in St George's Hall.

BRENTFORD AND CHISWICK – has a separate music department in charge of a qualified librarian. Sponsored the formation of a Recital Club which is also subsidized, and gramophone concerts are arranged.

BRIGHTON – over 2,000 records with fine recording equipment. Promote regular lunchtime recitals.

BRISTOL – 7,000 items. Printed catalogues were issued in 1959 but are now out of print. A music librarian is employed on salary grade A.P.T.II.

BURNLEY – the Massey Music Library with over 11,000 books and scores and nearly 3,000 records. A music librarian is employed on salary grade A.P.T.II and an annual grant is made from the Massey bequest. 850 sets of vocal music and 460 sets of orchestral music. Regular lists of additions issued with bibliographical notes.

CAMBERWELL – excellent recording equipment and nearly 5,000 records. Concerts are given regularly. A music librarian is employed on salary grade A.P.T.II plus two additional staff.

CARDIFF – a general collection of 6,000 volumes, specializing in Welsh music and music by Welsh composers. Has the Aylward collection of English sacred and organ music, and the Bonner Morgan collection of 17th- and 18th-century music, which includes ten mss volumes of early Italian operas, originally assembled at Gnoll Castle by Sir Henry Mackworth, 1766–1790.

CARLISLE – sponsors lunch-hour concerts held in the Art Gallery or the City Hall arranged by the Carlisle Arts Council.

CASTLEFORD – has 2,000 records with reproducing equipment and a soundproof room.

CHELSEA – 560 volumes of musical literature, 2,253 music scores including 450 miniature scores, and 590 records. Equipment consists of a Capitol stereo player and an Allen Inspecting machine.

CHELTENHAM – 2,212 items. Arranges lectures.

CHESHIRE – 2,030 items.

CHESTERFIELD – sets of choral and orchestral music. Organizes lectures and concerts. Has the advisory services of Dr G. F. Linstead and the committee responsible has the apt title of Library and Cultural Activities Committee.

COLCHESTER – record collection. Organizes concerts.

COVENTRY – 6,000 items and 6,356 records. Stereo equipment used for lunch-time recitals. A music librarian is employed on salary grade A.P.T.II.

DAGENHAM – 6,500 items and 3,660 records with fine reproducing equipment. Excellent catalogues of music and records are issued. Lectures and concerts are arranged and each of the four branch libraries has a piano. A music librarian is employed on salary grade A.P.T.I.

DEPTFORD – 3,500 records and reproducing equipment. Lectures and concerts are arranged, in conjunction with the Goldsmiths College Concert Society.

DERBYSHIRE – many choral sets. Quarterly lists of accessions are issued and sectional lists are in preparation. A music librarian is employed on salary grade A.P.T.I.

DORSET – 2,130 items and sets of scores.

DUDLEY – 3,000 items and 1,150 records, with reproducing equipment. Concerts and lectures are sponsored by the Dudley Arts Council of which the Borough Librarian and Borough Treasurer are Secretary and Treasurer respectively. The second edition of their gramophone record catalogue was published in October 1961.

DUNDEE – the A. J. Wighton collection of Scottish music, and rare English and Irish musical books. Autograph letters from German, French and British composers written to Wighton himself and a wide collection of folk-songs of all nations.

DURHAM – 7,000 items and issues music lists from time to time. Sets of orchestral music being purchased for use by societies within the county.

EASTBOURNE – a separate music department is included in their new central library opened in 1964. Has published a classified printed catalogue of music scores.

EAST RIDING – sets of choral music. Gramophone records. Catalogues published recently and now in process of revision.

EAST SUFFOLK – 2,000 records and sets of vocal and instrumental music. A Decca portable player is used.

EAST SUSSEX – 1,500 records and reproducing equipment. A record catalogue – the best I have yet seen – was issued in 1960 and is supplemented by annual lists. A music librarian is employed on a salary grade A.P.T.II.

EDINBURGH – 38,000 scores and books. Sets are collected and concerts are promoted in the Nelson Hall. A music librarian is employed plus two assistants.

ENFIELD – has 2,650 items, including 650 miniature scores, and 3,150 records. Equipment consists of a Garrard 301 motor, Quad acoustical stereo amplifiers, a Decca pick-up and Arundel speakers. Music lectures and concerts are arranged and a music librarian is employed on salary grade A.P.T.II with one general division assistant.

ESSEX – 33,000 items and 20,000 records, with a fine range of reproducing equipment. Sets of choral and instrumental music and stencilled lists issued periodically. One assistant on salary A.P.T.I. is in charge of the Music and Drama departments.

FINCHLEY – 5,016 items and 4,196 records. A Decca record player and a Pye Black box used in the Children's Library. Lunch hour gramophone recitals given and opera lecture recitals once or twice a year.

FULHAM – 4,800 items and 2,900 records. Wharfedale and Leak speakers, and Collaro and Studio pickups. A music librarian is employed on a salary of A.P.T.II with one general division assistant.

GILLINGHAM – 2,105 items. Stages record recitals on its Garrard turntable with Collaro pickup, a Quad II amplifier and Vitavox loudspeaker. A Vitavox Bitone reproducer is being purchased and additional equipment for conversion to stereophonic sound.

GLASGOW – the Music Room in the Mitchell Library was opened in 1930 and now has 30,000 works, including the Frank Kidson collection of 4,000 volumes of old music, folk-songs and folk-dances which was purchased in 1930. An opera collection of full scores, orchestral parts and vocal scores was presented by Charles Manners and Frank Moody in 1934. Smaller collections are those of Lady Gardiner (800 volumes), and Robert Turnbull (1,500 volumes). Two senior librarians are employed with extra assistants and music lectures are promoted.

GLOUCESTER – 2,761 items; is forming a record collection; has a Garrard motor, a Decca pickup, Leak amplifiers and two Quad electrostatic speakers. Record recitals of classical music and jazz, and music lectures are given and the city possesses the records of the stewards of the Three Choirs Festival dating back to the mid-18th century.

GREAT YARMOUTH – arranges concerts. A Pye player and a Blüthner grand piano.

GREENWICH – 4,346 items and 1,700 records with two Deccalian players. A Branch Librarian is given an additional grade on the A.P.T. scales because of special music duties, making the grade A.P.T.IV.

GRIMSBY – 1,100 items and 1,700 records. A Decca stereo pickup, Garrard transcription turntable with Quad amplifiers are used for recitals and G.E.C. Periphonic and Heathkit Cotswold speakers are used for public concerts in the Town Hall. AKC K.50 earphones have been installed for listening purposes in the library. A music librarian is employed graded A.P.T.II with one general division assistant. The new central library will have a separate music department.

GUILDFORD – a small collection which will be greatly enlarged in the new central library officially opened in October 1962. Activities in the borough are controlled by a Music Director who is responsible for concerts and recitals. A Song Index is maintained in sheaf catalogue form giving the titles and locations of over 5,000 compositions, both English and foreign.

HACKNEY – 2,779 items and 2,357 records. Expensive stereo equipment is provided, recitals are given regularly and a music librarian is employed graded A.P.T.II.

HAMILTON – a small collection of music and is building up a collection of records.

HAMMERSMITH – 5,150 items, 3,369 records and E.M.I. stereo equipment. Recitals are given and there is a printed catalogue.

HAMPSTEAD – 7,507 items and 7,500 records. Garrard equipment is provided and a staff of three is employed graded A.P.T.III, II and one person on the general division. Lists of additions covering records, books and scores are published regularly.

HARROGATE – 2,082 items and 450 records. A stencilled list of the records was issued in 1962.

HENDON – 4,760 items and 5,361 records. A new, separate music department was opened in 1961 and they also have a staff of three, graded as are those at Hampstead. The equipment comprises a Goldring Lenco motor with Tannoy pickup, a Quad 22 amplifier, 2 Vitavox speakers and Brown Type K moving-coil stick earphones. Lunch-time recitals are given.

HEREFORDSHIRE – a small collection of music, 2,000 records and a player. Records are paid for by the education authority who have the use of the collection free of charge for their associated bodies. Students may also borrow them freely but other persons pay an annual subscription. A record catalogue was published in 1961.

HERTFORDSHIRE – 12,550 items. The stock of the Hitchin Rural Music School is at present being absorbed into the county library's own collection.

HOLBORN – 4,708 items and 4,768 records, an E.M.G. stereo player for recitals which are held three times a week, and a listening cubicle gramophone. Recitals are also given in the wards of three London hospitals.

HORNSEY – 6,428 items including 1,395 miniature scores, and 2,870 records. A Garrard amplifier and Tannoy loudspeakers. A staff of two is employed, the senior person graded Clerical II. Lectures and recitals are given regularly and three orchestral concerts are provided in the Town Hall. Book lists on musical topics are issued regularly and there is an active gramophone society.

HOVE – 2,550 items including 300 miniature scores. Gramophone recitals are held weekly in the Museum and the Hangleton Branch Library.

HUDDERSFIELD – 60,000 items including a large collection of scores and parts both orchestral and vocal. There are also 1,402 records, stereo equipment, and regular concerts are sponsored by the Arts Committee. The town is internationally famous for its choral society which has given so many exciting performances at home and abroad over a long period.

HULL – 11,500 items and 3,500 records. Stereo equipment with a Goldring Lenco turntable and pickup, and Wharfedale speakers. A music librarian is employed graded A.P.T.II with one full-time general division assistant and one part-time assistant. Music lectures and concerts are arranged.

ISLE OF WIGHT – a small music collection and 1,045 records which are purchased from Further Education Funds. Catalogues of music scores and records have been issued in stencilled form.

KEIGHLEY – a small collection of records and music. A Farnell stereo player, Bean Echo speakers and a tape recorder.

KENDAL/WESTMORLAND – 3,250 items and 300 records. The classification arrangement is that of the British Catalogue of Music.

KENSINGTON – 4,750 items, 4,600 records, a Philco monarch player and a Blüthner concert grand in Leighton House for concerts. Staff consists of two assistants, one graded A.P.T.I.

KENT – 12,800 items including 1,200 orchestral and vocal sets. A librarian graded A.P.T.II is in charge of the Music and Drama section with two assistants.

KETTERING – 2,218 items. Arranges record recitals.

LAMBETH – 9,650 items ; 9,000 records ; Decca equipment and gives lunch-hour recitals.

LANARKSHIRE – 7,284 items and started a record library in 1962.

LANCASHIRE – 4,400 items and a post of Music and Drama Librarian. A printed list of additions is issued.

LANCASTER – has the J. A. Fuller Maitland collection which was acquired in the 1930s. He was the editor of *Grove's Dictionary* and his collection consists of several thousand items. Part of the collection is on temporary loan to the University of Liverpool but the remainder is neither catalogued nor available to the public. As one of the new University towns, the local authority will surely bestir itself to house this collection adequately, make its contents known and its use possible.

LEEDS – 27,975 items including orchestral sets, 6,000 long-play records, a Quad II amplifier with Connoisseur pick-up and Wharfedale Speakers. There are six staff, one graded A.P.T.II, one A.P.T.I and four assistants. Record recitals are given and the Music Committee arranges midday and Saturday concerts. A monthly list of gramophone records and an orchestral musical catalogue are published. Over 600 items are of 18th-century music, many of which were bought in 1905 at the sale of the William Tophouse collection.

LEICESTER – 3,415 items.

LEICESTERSHIRE – 3,898 items, 1,047 records and a Bush player. The County Education Committee pays for the record library which is for use by schools only.

LEWISHAM – 3,588 items in its central library, collections at the branch libraries, 9,017 records, a Deccola radiogram, a Deccalian portable and a Leak amplifier with separate turntables and a Tannoy York speaker. Four upright pianos are used by cultural societies. A music librarian is graded A.P.T.III and has two assistants. Lectures and concerts are staged.

LEYTON – 3,482 items and three record players, comprising a City Electrical installation, a Deccalian portable and a specially built player given by Reliance Cords and Cables Ltd. A Cramer upright piano is used and concerts are a regular feature. A Vortexion tape recorder is used for the growing collection of pre-recorded tapes.

LINCOLN – 690 volumes of music literature, 1,200 scores and 250 miniature scores. Concerts are given in the Art Gallery and a grant of £150 made from a local fund towards their cost. A Blüthner grand piano is used.

LINDSEY AND HOLLAND – 5,000 items, 2,650 records including 650 long players and a Bush player. A record catalogue has been published.

LIVERPOOL – exciting developments here. The old music library established in 1859, was completely destroyed in May 1941 and a temporary service had to be established. In 1959 however, the new suite was opened by Sir Arthur Bliss and it consists of an entrance foyer, a periodicals foyer, a concert room to seat 100, the library proper, a music mss exhibition foyer, a gramophone listening room and records collection and a stockroom. Professional and amateur societies throughout the country are subscribing members to the library and a printed dictionary catalogue of music was produced in 1954. The library has 40,000 volumes of music on its open shelves, miniature and full scores, over 10,000 items of music literature and room for 100,000 items in the stack. Its musical rarities include medieval illuminated mss and original letters and mss of Verdi, Rossini, Schubert, Weber, Paganini and Haydn. There are 4,000 records, Garrard and Dynatron players and an Allison upright piano. A staff of six administers the collections. Sets of music can be borrowed by city societies for a subscription of one guinea and by non-resident bodies for 2 guineas per annum.

LLANELLY – 3,620 items, 4,200 records including 2,000 long plays, a Garrard transcription motor with a Decca pick-up, two Goodman speakers, a Ferrograph and a Grundig tape recorder. A record catalogue is issued.

MANCHESTER – Henry Watson Music Library. Was deposited with the Corporation in 1899 and is one of the most comprehensive collections in existence. The original nucleus consisted of 16,700 volumes including 2,500 books about music. There are now 8,500 books, over 90,000 scores, plus 320,000 separate musical pieces. Forty-six musical periodicals are currently taken and there are over 2,000 volumes of bound periodicals. Subscriptions can be taken out by institutions and societies outside the city for a modest sum, at present 2½ guineas. The aims are to help equally the lonely student and the flourishing society, the orchestra enthusiast and the lover of chamber music, the general reader and the research scholar. To facilitate the arrangement of programmes, choral and orchestral works can be reserved six months in advance. It is the largest library of its kind in the world and lends 150,000 items of choral and orchestral music annually. The complete editions of Breitkopf and Härtel, the publications of the more important societies and over 400 rarities are other valuable

possessions. A staff of five administers the library, one graded
A.P.T.III, one A.P.T.II and three assistants.

MANSFIELD – 3,326 items, 2,500 records, a Deccola player and a
Cramer piano. Lectures and concerts are arranged and a record
catalogue is published.

MIDDLESEX – 5,260 titles with multiple copies of books and scores
at the 40 branch libraries, 2,750 records and record players at
various centres. Concerts are arranged and a music librarian
grade A.P.T.II is in charge at Headquarters.

MOTHERWELL AND WISHAW – 1,095 items, 1,630 records including
770 long plays, and a Decca player. An excellent home-produced
record catalogue is published.

NEATH – has a very small music collection and 1,480 records with
Trixette equipment.

NEWARK – has a very small collection of music and records which is
at present undergoing enlargement.

NEWCASTLE-UNDER-LYME – 1,300 items and 1,000 records.

NEWCASTLE-UPON-TYNE – 17,500 items including 1,500 miniature
scores. The new Central Library will have a separate music department and whilst the provision of records has been approved
in principle, it cannot be implemented in the present building
owing to lack of space. Newcastle has issued some superlative
music lists of recent date. 'Miniature Scores' was first published
in 1953 and revised in 1958; 'Piano Scores' was issued in 1954 and
revised in 1959; 'Songs' 1955; 'Organ Music' 1956. These are all
printed lists. A handlist of recorder music was published in 1959.

NORTHAMPTON – 2,050 items.

NORWICH – 3,344 items.

NOTTINGHAM – 3,650 items, 1,000 records and a Bush player. A
music librarian, degreed, is graded A.P.T.II.

NOTTINGHAMSHIRE – 13,650 items including 1,300 choral and 200
orchestral sets which are borrowed by 165 affiliated groups. A
music librarian is graded A.P.T.I and an annual printed catalogue of sets of choral music is issued in a handy pocket size.

Valuable catalogues have been produced of miniature, vocal and piano scores, choral, instrumental and orchestral music.

ORKNEY – a small collection, including 400 long-play records; arranges recitals using the equipment of the County Music Organizer.

PADDINGTON – 3,850 items whilst PEMBROKESHIRE has about 2,850 items and 981 records.

PENGE – 2,260 items, 488 long plays and 1,152 records at 78 r.p.m. Lectures and concerts are arranged, and there is a B.S.R. player with a Leak amplifier.

PETERBOROUGH – a small collection of 1,652 items.

PLYMOUTH – over 11,000, including 350 orchestral sets. A Pye Hi-Fi Console model and a beautiful Steinway grand are used for lectures and concerts. A Music and Drama Librarian is graded A.P.T.II and has one assistant. A catalogue of part songs and oratorios has been published and a second catalogue of orchestral parts is in preparation. The Music Library also maintains the Diary of Musical Events for the town.

POPLAR – 1,286 items, 1,617 records and a Murphy portable player.

PRESTON – 4,358 items.

READING – 4,450 items, 832 records and a Deccalian player. Selective booklists are published frequently and a monthly list of record additions is issued.

RICHMOND (SURREY) – 2,754 items and ROCHDALE 2,960. Concerts and lectures are arranged here.

ROCHESTER – 1,870 items, 1,300 records including 500 long plays. Concerts and lectures are arranged by the local music society.

ROTHERHAM – 3,050 items whilst ROTHWELL (Yorkshire) has only a small collection but 1,786 records with a Phillips player and speaker.

ST ALBANS – 1,465 and ST HELENS 2,222 items but the latter is about to commence a record library.

ST MARYLEBONE – 10,700 items including 1,650 miniature scores and 3,308 long-play records. Equipment consists of a Deccalian portable for testing and a Connoisseur player for recitals with Quad amplifier and speaker. The music librarian is graded A.P.T.III, an assistant is A.P.T.II and there are two other assistants. A monthly list of recent record additions is published and cumulated three times a year. The music collections are drawn upon by personnel of the Royal Academy of Music and Trinity College, both within the Borough.

ST PANCRAS – 2,882 items and 4,490 records including 2,490 long plays. The equipment is a Collaro 2,010 transcription unit with an R.D. junior amplifier and a Wharfedale speaker. The music librarian is graded A.P.T.II and has one assistant. Lectures and concerts are a regular feature.

SALE – 1,470, SALFORD – 1,702, SCARBOROUGH – 1,630 items are small by comparison with others, but at the Yorkshire resort, concerts are arranged in co-operation with the University of Hull and a Bechstein concert grand is used from time to time.

SCUNTHORPE – only 800 items but 2,500 records and the collections are being expanded. A Dansette player is used for recitals, a printed catalogue is issued and a qualified librarian is in charge of the collections.

SHEFFIELD – 5,359 items including 890 miniature scores. There are 250 records and the equipment consists of an Avantis amplifier with Lemco Deck; Garrard and Strobescope players. Record recitals are held.

SHOREDITCH – 2,270 items and 1,958 records including 1,533 long plays and some stereos. A Collaro player is used for lunch-time recitals but at present, only societies may borrow discs. A stencilled catalogue is available.

SHROPSHIRE – 23,818 items, 1,771 records including 960 long plays and a Clarke and Smith player. The County Library is a depository for local societies and the music and drama librarian is graded A.P.T.II. Records are held by H.Q. and three branches, and it is a developing service so far as the branches are concerned. It is interesting to note that the gramophone collection was started by a local Trust and now includes language discs, and that the Trust also bought the equipment and printed the catalogue. A catalogue of the extensive collection of sheet music has also been issued.

SHREWSBURY and SOLIHULL – small collections.

SOMERSET – 7,283 items and is developing its collection.

SOUTHAMPTON – 4,150 items. Lectures and concerts are held in the Art Gallery and the Guildhall organized by the Education Committee, the W.E.A. and the Entertainments Department respectively.

SOUTHEND – 3,365 items and SOUTHWARK – 1,300. The Metropolitan borough also has 3,300 records, all but 300 of them long plays, and both monaural and stereo equipment is provided. The gramophone record librarian is graded A.P.T.II/III and has one assistant. Printed subject lists of records and additions lists are issued irregularly.

STAFFORDSHIRE – 7,794 items including 1,275 miniature scores and a record library commenced on 1st April, 1962. Sets of music are collected and the music and drama librarian is graded A.P.T.II. A new edition of the music catalogue was published in 1962.

STEPNEY – 4,820 items, 5,471 records including 1,234 long plays and the equipment comprises a record deck and amplifier, 2 Dansette players and 1 Pye player and recorder. Lunch-time record recitals are given.

STOCKPORT – 6,650 items whilst STOKE NEWINGTON has 1,651 items, 1,200 long plays, an H.M.V. capitol stereo player and a Wallis piano. The record librarian is graded A.P.T.I.

STOKE-ON-TRENT – 3,596 items; STRETFORD – 1,469 items and arranges a concert programme.

SURBITON – 1,670 items.

SURREY – collection numbers 53,650 including over 2,000 miniature and full scores. An extensive collection of vocal and orchestral sets is held and two excellent catalogues were issued in 1960. The music and drama librarian is graded A.P.T.I.

SUTTON AND CHEAM – 3,501 items and 2,925 records with a Decca player. One assistant paid on the general division is in charge with an additional payment of £40 for special duties.

SUTTON-IN-ASHFIELD – a small collection including 604 records.

4

SWANSEA – 2,400 items and 4,000 records. Concerts are arranged and equipment includes a Trixette player and a Garrard Deck with Pamphonic amplifier and speakers. A record librarian is graded in the general division.

SWINDON – 2,465 items and 430 records lent only to societies. Equipment is both monaural and stereophonic; there is a Deccalian player, a tape recorder and two pianos including a Blüthner grand. Music flourishes here and the library sponsors a music club and a gramophone society, and organizes chamber music and symphony concerts. £1,000 is set aside for expenditure on these activities and a contribution is made to the expenses of the Bournemouth symphony orchestra.

SWINTON AND PENDLEBURY – 2,400 items and a Steinway grand. TORQUAY – 1,600; TUNBRIDGE WELLS – 1,418 and a Scheidman piano. Music lectures are held here.

TOTTENHAM – 5,730 items including 800 miniature scores, 1,700 records, and a Pye Blackbox player. Staff consists of a librarian-in-charge graded A.P.T.III; a Senior Assistant A.P.T.II and two assistants A.P.T.I. A song index on cards lists items not in Sears.

TWICKENHAM – 4,025 items: WAKEFIELD – 2,868; WALLASEY – 5,130 and WALSALL – 2,120.

WALTHAMSTOW – 6,030 items, 3,500 records, a Garrard turntable with Collaro pickup, Spectone amplifiers and dual speakers. Record recitals are given. A Grade III assistant is in charge of special activities and has one full-time assistant dealing with gramophone records.

WANDSWORTH – is to build a new music department shortly at Balham to house its 4,840 items and 6,500 records. A record player is used for recitals and staff consists of one senior graded A.P.T.II and two assistants. Duplicated catalogues of records have been published.

WARWICKSHIRE – 5,130 items; WARRINGTON – 3,154 with a collection of orchestral parts and WATFORD – 2,996.

WEST HAM – 5,180 items including 768 miniature scores and 1,300 records the property of the Education Committee lent only to accredited organizations. A Deccola player is used for recitals and lectures, and excellent catalogues have been issued recently of their miniature scores and gramophone records. The branch librarian at Canning Town is the music librarian and is graded A.P.T.III.

WEST RIDING – $\frac{1}{4}$ million items; the gramophone record collection is administered directly by the Education Committee. Catalogues are issued of choral, instrumental and brass band music, the latter particularly appropriate to the county of Yorkshire. An extensive collection of musical sets is well used by societies in the county and the Yorkshire Regional Library System.

WEST SUFFOLK – 1,360 items and 700 records. Developments are planned in the near future.

WEST SUSSEX – has 10,500 items and 3,150 records of which only 150 are long players. These are lent to societies and schools only. Catalogues of the music collection have been published in six parts.

WESTMINSTER – the Westminster City Council has an impressive collection housed in two buildings. The Central Music Library Ltd, in Buckingham Palace Road, S.W.1 is unique. It was formed in 1946 and is primarily a lending library. The extensive stock is the property of the Central Music Library Co., deposited on long-term loan, housed and administered by the City Council. There are 45,000 items and a further 33,000 from the Westminster Public Libraries stock are amalgamated with them. The basic elements in the library are the collections of Edwin Evans and Gerald Cooper. A gift of £10,000 for purchases was made by Mrs Winifred Christie Moore and assistance has been given by the Arts Council, the British Council and the Vaughan Williams Trust. There is a good representation of old English and Italian music, and also of modern British, French, and Russian composers. The collected works of many composers are available on loan including Bach's Gesellschaft, Purcell, Beethoven, Brahms, Handel's Arnold edition, Mozart, Tschaikovsky and Rimsky-Korsakov. There are bound volumes of the back numbers of numerous periodicals, both English and foreign. Any person from anywhere with a current public library ticket, can borrow from the music library and it serves a real need. The staff includes the

music librarian graded A.P.T.III, one senior assistant graded
A.P.T.II and one general division assistant.

The gramophone record library and the collection of miniature
scores are to be found at 4 Charing Cross Road, W.C.2. Here are
16,904 discs, including 7,981 long plays and 2,548 language
records. A Collaro monaural record player is used for testing
purposes and I believe for music-while-you-work sessions too!
There is a librarian in charge graded A.P.T.II, and two general
division assistants.

WIDNES – 2,050 items and 1,100 long plays with a Pye player.
Lectures are held.

WIGAN – 5,830 items, 1,000 records, an Alba player and a Hansen
piano. A senior assistant, employed part time on music duties, is
graded A.P.T.II and has one full-time assistant.

WILTSHIRE – 3,312 items and 1,650 records lent only to societies
and schools. Sets of choral music are collected and catalogues have
been issued of these together with long playing and 78 r.p.m.
records.

WILLESDEN – 2,775 items and WOLVERHAMPTON – 3,246 with a
Chappell piano.

WOOLWICH – 2,200 items and 3,000 records with two Deccalian
players and mss scores of Ladislas Joseph Philip Paul Zavertal,
conductor of the Royal Artillery Band, 1881–1906.

WORCESTERSHIRE – 1,125 items and 867 choral sets which are
selected by the County Music Organizer and paid for out of
Education Funds.

WORKINGTON – 648 items and 1,300 records with a Bush stereo
player. Concerts are arranged by the local Arts Club which
receives a grant from the Council. Tape recorders are used to
record local musical events, an unusual innovation, and a very
commendable one.

WORTHING – 1,457 items and an uncatalogued collection of 2,000
orchestral and choral works.

YORK – 3,151 items including 422 miniature scores.

BRITISH PUBLIC LIBRARIES

(selected)

STOCKS OF MUSIC AND MUSIC LITERATURE

STATISTICAL TABLE

These tables show the books on music, scores, miniature scores and full scores. Gramophone records are analysed wherever possible into long play, extended play, short play and 78 r.p.m. In some cases, only a total figure can be given as the numbers of the various categories are unknown. This applies also to stocks of music literature which again, in a few libraries, is not recorded separately.

Place	Musical Literature	Scores	M/ Scores	Full Scores	Total	L.P.	E.P.	S.P.	78	Total
ABERDEEN	1,798	1,285	241	27	**3,351**	–	–	–	–	–
ACCRINGTON	600	2,000	–	–	**2,600**	–	–	–	–	–
AYR	cannot be given	200	30	–	**230**	–	–	–	–	–
BARROW-IN-FURNESS	413	1,464	–	60	**1,937**	\	–	–	–	–

Place	Musical Literature	Scores	M/ Scores	Full Scores	Total	L.P.	E.P.	S.P.	78	Total
BATTERSEA	1,050	2,125	360	25	3,560	1,400	50	2,690	–	4,140
BEBINGTON	360	625	70	–	1,055	–	–	–	–	650
BECKENHAM	535	1,381	323	–	2,239	–	–	–	–	1,000
BEDDINGTON AND WALLINGTON	622	1,391	232	10	2,245	–	–	–	–	–
BEDFORD	521	1,620	223	4	2,368	–	–	–	–	–
BERMONDSEY	545	1,314	117	–	1,976	–	–	–	–	4,242
BETHNAL GREEN	600	1,200	600	14	2,414	–	–	–	–	1,770
BEXLEY	621	1,000	47	24	1,692	–	–	–	–	–
BIRKENHEAD	790	1,450	100	–	2,340	–	–	–	–	–
BIRMINGHAM	4,530	11,440	1,580	200	17,750	–	–	–	–	–
BLACKBURN	475	750	145	60	1,830	–	–	–	–	300
BLACKPOOL	300	1,267	243	40	1,850	–	–	–	–	–

					Total				Planned for 1964-5
BOOTLE	613	1,391	50	40	**2,094**	–	–	–	–
BOURNEMOUTH	2,000	5,000	600	400	**8,000**	–	–	–	–
BRADFORD	1,445	7,814	1,729	333	**11,321**	–	–	——— planned in new building ———	–
BRENTFORD AND CHISWICK	974	1,468	459	2	**2,903**	–	–	–	**1,500**
BRIGHTON	810	2,565	480	–	**3,855**	–	–	–	**2,091**
BRISTOL	1,894	3,901	875	228	**6,898**	–	–	–	–
BROMLEY	667	662	156	–	**1,485**	–	–	–	**800**
BUCKS	——— cannot be given ———								
BURNLEY	{	–	–	–	**11,116**	859	1,888	–	**2,747**
					also sets of choral and orchestral music				
BURTON-UPON-TRENT	600	900	75	–	**1,575**	–	–	–	–
CAMBERWELL	1,353	1,616	965	–	**3,934**	–	–	–	**4,624**
CAMBRIDGE	600	1,400	300	30	**2,330**	–	–	–	–
CANTERBURY	83	316	95	–	**494**	–	–	–	–
CARDIFF	4,000	6,714	1,424	613	**12,751**	–	–	2,500	**2,500**

Place	Musical Literature	Scores	M/ Scores	Full Scores	Total	L.P.	E.P.	S.P.	78	Total
CARLISLE	1,006	2,086	245	23	3,360	—	—	—	—	—
CARSHALTON	700	1,140	260	—	1,400	—	—	—	—	—
CASTLEFORD	300	1,150	60	18	1,528	—	—	—	—	1,970
CHELMSFORD	650	8,524	30	1,515	10,719	—	—	—	—	—
CHELSEA	560	1,803 also sets of choral music	450	—	2,813	590	—	—	—	590
CHELTENHAM	632	1,368	204	8	2,212	—	—	—	—	—
CHESTERFIELD	600	1,400	200	—	2,221 also sets of choral and orchestral music	—	—	—	—	—
CLACKMANNAN	125	487	112	—	724	—	—	—	152	152
CLYDEBANK	482	800	94	—	1,376	—	—	—	—	30
COLCHESTER	200	600	200	—	1,000	—	—	—	—	1,654
COULSDON AND PURLEY	1,331	2,737	425	50	4,543	—	—	—	—	—

COVENTRY	890	2,550	900	1,650	5,990	–	–	–	–	6,356
CREWE	256	591	54	–	901	339	39	–	445	823
CROYDON	——— cannot be given ———						–	–	–	1,500
DAGENHAM	1,500	4,000	1,000	–	6,500	1,750	150	–	1,763	3,663
DEPTFORD	750	1,500	250	–	2,500	–	–	–	–	3,500
DERBY	651	1,416	163	–	2,230	–	–	–	–	–
DERBYSHIRE	1,386	11,699	765	–	13,850	–	–	–	–	–
DEVON	1,400	2,200	280	150	4,030	–	–	–	–	–
DEWSBURY	500	1,450	200	–	2,150	–	–	–	–	–
DONCASTER	494	1,125	475	–	2,094	–	–	–	–	–
DORSET COUNTY	2,130	–	–	–	2,130	–	–	–	–	–
DOVER	196	843	98	–	1,137	–	–	–	–	–
DUDLEY	1,020	1,820	400	–	3,240	–	–	–	–	1,150
DUNDEE	920	2,650	250	12	3,832	–	–	–	–	–
DURHAM COUNTY	1,500	5,000	450	40	6,990	–	–	–	–	–

4*

Place	Musical Litera-ture	Scores	M/ Scores	Full Scores	Total	L.P.	E.P.	S.P.	78	Total
EALING	960	1,750	209	6	2,925	–	–	–	–	–
EASTBOURNE	550	900	350	–	1,800	–	–	–	–	–
EAST RIDING	800	2,700	100	–	3,600	–	–	–	–	400
		Sets of choral music								
EAST SUFFOLK	Sets of ch. and inst. music		140	–	140	2,000	–	–	–	2,000
EAST SUSSEX	800	1,600	420	–	2,820	–	–	–	–	1,500
EDINBURGH	–	–	–	–	38,000	–	–	–	–	–
ELLESMERE PORT	150	375	50	–	575	–	–	–	–	912
ENFIELD	500	1,500	650	–	2,650	3,150	–	–	–	3,150
ERITH	400	530	18	–	948	–	–	–	–	–
		Sets of choral music								
ESSEX	5,000	27,000	1,250	200	33,450	–	–	–	–	19,730
			Sets of choral and orchestral music							

FINCHLEY	580	3,402	1,034	–	**5,016**	–	–	–	–	–	–
FINSBURY	750	1,576	246	–	**2,572**	1,097	–	–	–	3,099	4,196
FOLKESTONE	750	650	–	–	**1,400**	–	–	–	–	–	–
FULHAM	4,200	–	600	–	**4,800**	2,900	–	–	–	–	2,900
GATESHEAD	612	1,207	112	–	**1,931**	–	–	–	–	–	–
GILLINGHAM	570	1,200	335	–	**2,105**	–	–	–	–	–	–
GLOUCESTER	871	1,528	362	–	**2,761**	–	–	–	–	–	–
GLASGOW	17,000	33,300	1,240	460	**50,000**	–	–	–	–	–	–
GREAT YARMOUTH	525	500	–	–	**1,025**	–	–	–	–	–	–
GREENOCK	500	400	–	–	**900**	–	–	–	–	–	–
GREENWICH	1,342	2,320	684	–	**4,346**	–	–	–	–	–	7,184
GRIMSBY	350	400	350	–	**1,100**	2,000	–	–	–	–	2,000
GUILDFORD	432	575	22	5	**1,025**	–	–	–	–	–	–
HACKNEY	971	1,371	437	–	**2,779**	2,257	–	–	–	–	2,357
HALIFAX	627	1,478	55	1	**2,161**	–	–	–	–	–	–

Place	Musical Litera- ture	Scores	M/ Scores	Full Scores	Total	L.P.	E.P.	S.P.	78	Total
HAMILTON	550	585	58	18	1,211	67	–	–	–	67
HAMMERSMITH	1,000	3,000	1,100	50	5,150	3,369	–	–	–	3,369
HAMPSTEAD	1,500	4,500	1,500	7	7,507	2,000	–	–	5,500	7,500
HARROGATE	600	1,200	250	30	2,080	450	–	–	–	450
HENDON	1,250	2,700	600	210	4,760	4,501	–	–	860	5,361
HEREFORDSHIRE	800	1,675	200	–	2,675	2,000	–	–	–	2,000
HERTFORDSHIRE	2,050	9,200	1,300	–	12,550	–	–	–	–	–
HOLBORN	1,784	2,924	–	–	4,708	–	–	–	–	5,377
HORNSEY	1,574	3,459	1,395	–	6,428	2,870	–	–	–	2,870
HOUNSLOW	970	1,910	162	–	3,042	–	–	–	–	–
HOVE	1,350	2,550	300	–	4,200	–	–	–	–	–
HUDDERSFIELD	1,644	54,895	573	124	57,236	–	–	–	–	–

HULL	3,500	7,000	1,000	–	11,500	3,500	–	–	3,500
IPSWICH	1,111	1,300	180	50	2,641	–	–	–	–
ISLE OF WIGHT	1,500	1,200	100	–	2,800	–	–	–	–
ISLINGTON	600	1,000	–	–	1,600	–	–	–	–
KEIGHLEY	583	884	277	303	2,047	15	–	–	15
KENDAL	1,000	2,000	250	–	3,250	300	–	–	300
KENSINGTON	750	4,000	–	–	4,750	4,600	–	–	4,600
KENT	2,000	9,200	1,500	100	12,800	–	–	–	–
KETTERING	595	1,394	229	–	2,218	–	–	–	–
KIDDERMINSTER	573	1,164	117	18	1.836	–	–	–	–
LAMBETH	3,600	6,050	–	–	9,650	9,000	–	–	9,000
LANARK	3,953	2,727	459	145	7,284	–	–	–	–
LEAMINGTON SPA	439	898	20	–	1,357	–	–	–	–
LEEDS	6,190	17,739	3,240	806	27,975	–	–	–	–
LEICESTER	1,615	1,400	400	100	3,415	–	–	–	–

Place	Musical Litera-ture	Scores	M/Scores	Full Scores	Total	L.P.	E.P.	S.P.	78	Total
LEICESTERSHIRE	1,011	1,964	570	353	3,898	–	–	–	–	–
LEWISHAM	1,015	1,306	1,224	43	3,588	9,017	–	–	–	9,017
LEYTON	642	2,361	479	–	3,482	–	–	–	–	–
LINDSAY AND HOLLAND C.	1,000	3,500	500	–	5,000	650	–	–	2,000	2,650
LIVERPOOL	10,000	40,000	1,800	1,200	53,000	4,000	–	–	–	4,000
LLANELLY	900	2,000	700	20	3,620	2,200	–	–	2,000	4,200
MANCHESTER	7,000	300,000	4,300	2,100	313,400	–	–	–	–	–
MANSFIELD	1,870	1,355	100	1	3,326	2,500	–	–	–	2,500
MIDDLESBROUGH	1,273	2,715	988	96	5,072	–	–	–	–	–
MIDDLESEX	1,650	2,970	401	139	5,260	2,570	–	–	–	2,570
MITCHAM	529	1,904	246	12	2,691	–	–	–	–	–
MOTHERWELL AND WISHAW	340	680	75	–	1,095	770	–	–	860	1,630
NEATH	160	–	330	–	490	1,480	–	–	–	1,480

NEWARK	100	150	60	—	310	112	—	—	—	112
NEWCASTLE-UNDER-LYME	1,300	—	—	—	1,300	500	—	—	—	500
NEWCASTLE-UPON-TYNE	2,500	13,500	1,500	—	17,500	—	—	—	—	—
NORTHAMPTON	650	1,150	200	50	2,050	—	—	—	—	—
NORWICH	873	2,122	324	25	3,344	—	—	—	—	—
NOTTINGHAM	700	2,200	700	50	3,650	1,000	—	—	—	1,000
NOTTINGHAMSHIRE	2,260	9,700	1,440	250	13,650	—	—	—	—	—
ORKNEY	200	50	—	—	250	400	—	—	—	400
ORPINGTON	1,166	723	98	—	1,987	—	—	—	—	—
OXFORDSHIRE	800	—	—	—	800	—	—	—	—	—
PADDINGTON	700	2,400	750	450	3,850	—	—	—	—	—
PEMBROKESHIRE	1,550	490	40	—	2,530	981	—	—	—	981
PENGE	400	1,400	460	—	2,260	488	—	—	1,152	1,640
PETERBOROUGH	530	1,064	58	—	1,652	—	—	—	—	—
PLYMOUTH	1,500	8,500	1,000	350	11,350	—	—	—	—	—

Place	Musical Literature	Scores	M/ Scores	Full Scores	Total	L.P.	E.P.	S.P.	78	Total
POPLAR	1,286	–	–	–	1,286	1,617	–	–	–	1,617
PRESTON	917	2,857	584	–	4,358	–	–	–	–	–
READING	1,171	2,603	676	–	4,450	832	–	–	–	832
RICHMOND (SURREY)	892	1,480	382	40	2,754	–	–	–	–	–
ROCHDALE	450	2,250	220	–	2,960	–	–	–	–	–
ROCHESTER	420	1,320	130	–	1,870	800	–	–	500	1,300
ROTHERHAM	1,000	1,700	350	–	3,050	4	–	–	–	4
ROTHWELL	266	515	24	–	805	1,786	–	–	–	1,786
ST ALBANS	256	859	52	298	1,465	–	–	–	–	–
ST HELENS	400	1,682	140	–	2,222	–	–	–	–	–
ST MARYLEBONE	2,500	6,550	1,650	–	10,700	3,308	–	–	–	3,308
ST PANCRAS	2,882	–	–	–	2,882	2,490	–	–	2,000	4,900

SALE	250	1,020	—	200	1,470	—	—	—	—	—
SALFORD	470	888	36	308	1,702	—	—	—	—	—
SCARBOROUGH	520	1,050	40	20	1,630	—	—	—	—	—
SCUNTHORPE	300	300	200	—	800	2,500	—	—	—	2,500
SHEFFIELD	755	3,714	890	—	5,359	250	—	—	—	250
SHOREDITCH	600	1,300	370	—	2,270	1,533	—	—	424	1,957
SHREWSBURY	320	350	60	—	730	—	—	—	—	—
SHROPSHIRE	3,158	19,654	196	10	23,818	960	—	—	811	1,771
SOLIHULL	757	607	206	20	1,590	—	—	—	—	—
SOMERSET	2,994	4,149	160	—	7,283	—	—	—	—	—
SOUTHAMPTON	2,100	2,000	350	—	4,450	—	—	—	—	—
SOUTHEND	1,315	1,900	150	—	3,365	—	—	—	—	—
SOUTHWARK	1,300	—	—	—	1,300	3,000	—	—	300	3,300
SPENBOROUGH	215	874	—	—	1,089	—	—	—	—	—
STAFFORD	450	253	115	—	818	—	—	—	—	—

Place	Musical Litera-ture	Scores	M/ Scores	Full Scores	Total	L.P.	E.P.	S.P.	78	Total
STAFFORDSHIRE	1,471	4,745	1,275	303	7,794	–	–	–	–	–
STEPNEY	2,000	2,120	700	–	4,820	1,234	487	–	3,750	5,471
STOCKPORT	1,000	5,000	600	50	6,650	–	–	–	–	–
STOKE NEWINGTON	1,651	–	–	–	1,651	1,200	–	–	–	1,200
STOKE-ON-TRENT	1,680	1,617	295	4	3,596	–	–	–	–	–
STRETFORD	480	952	32	5	1,469	–	–	–	–	–
SURBITON	500	1,020	150	–	1,670	–	–	–	–	–
SURREY	4,591	46,814	1,864	381	53,650	–	–	–	–	–
SUTTON AND CHEAM	3,501	–	–	–	3,501	2,925	–	–	–	2,925
SUTTON IN ASHFIELD	110	369	30	–	509	604	–	–	–	604
SWANSEA	500	1,300	600	–	2,400	4,000	–	–	–	4,000
SWINDON	2,069	938	458	–	3,465	430	–	–	–	430

SWINTON AND PENDLEBURY	586	1,452	362	—	2,400	—	—	—	—
TORQUAY	600	700	300	—	1,600	—	—	—	—
TOTTENHAM	1,100	3,780	800	50	6,180	1,700	—	—	1,700
TUNBRIDGE WELLS	380	739	222	77	1,418	—	—	—	—
TWICKENHAM	1,137	2,811	77	—	4,025	—	—	—	—
WAKEFIELD	402	1,405	38	23	2,868	—	—	—	—
WALLASEY	980	3,800	350	—	5,130	—	—	—	—
WALSALL	1,000	1,000	120	—	2,120	—	—	—	—
WALTHAMSTOW	1,400	3,400	1,200	30	6,030	3,500	—	—	3,500
WANDSWORTH	1,100	2,850	822	70	4,840	6,500	—	—	6,500
WARWICKSHIRE	3,800	1,150	100	80	5,130	—	—	—	—
WARRINGTON	700	2,279	175	—	3,154	—	—	—	—
WATFORD	2,996	—	—	—	2,996	—	—	—	—
WEST HAM	1,660	2,700	768	52	5,180	1,300	—	—	1,300

Place	Musical Litera-ture	Scores	M/ Scores	Full Scores	Total	L.P.	E.P.	S.P.	78	Total
WEST RIDING	5,700	250,000	–	–	255,700	–	–	–	–	–
WEST SUFFOLK	775	525	60	–	1,360	700	–	–	–	700
WEST SUSSEX	2,000	8,000	500	–	10,500	150	–	–	3,000	3,150
WIDNES	550	1,200	300	–	2,050	1,150	–	–	–	1,100
WIGAN	950	4,530	300	50	5,830	1,000	–	–	–	1,000
WILTSHIRE	1,100	1,800	400	12	3,312	1,650	–	–	–	1,650
WILLESDEN	1,000	913	793	69	2,775	–	–	–	–	–
WOLVERHAMPTON	607	2,080	307	252	3,246	–	–	–	–	–
WOOLWICH	520	1,250	450	–	2,220	3,000	–	–	–	3,000
WORKINGTON	143	493	12	–	648	1,300	–	–	–	1,300
WORTHING	536	828	93	–	1,457	–	–	–	–	–
YORK	778	1,953	422	16	3,151	–	–	–	–	–

8

British University and Special Libraries

ABERDEEN: University Library. 829 volumes of music literature, 16,959 scores, 1,310 miniature scores, 533 full scores and 3,219 gramophone records. The University is well equipped with 12 record players and 9 pianos. The music resources are divided between the Music Department Library at Marischal College and the general library at King's College. Many musical works were acquired by the copyright privileges possessed by the University in the early part of the 19th century. A catalogue of the W. L. Taylor collection of psalm books was issued in 1921.

ABERYSTWYTH: National Library of Wales. A copyright library which has an ever-growing collection of general musical literature. This now comprises 6,500 works, 58,850 scores and the special collection of Welsh music and music by Welsh composers which has some 6,600 items. The library of Congress classification scheme is used but sheet music is now arranged alphabetically by composer. Early manuscripts include a Supplementary Antiphonary and Office Book compiled by Father Peter Martyr Regalia, a singer in an Italian Dominican Monastery c. 1595–1622; music for the lute composed by Dr Francis Pilkington, 1595 and a collection of glees, rounds and catches by 17th-century composers. Non-copyright material is lent.

BIRMINGHAM: University Library. An extensive collection, with Sir Edward Elgar well represented, as he was the first professor of music here.

BURNHAM: Buckinghamshire – Hashdom Abbey. A library of church music, musical and liturgical history of about 1,200 volumes up to A.D. 1600 and 1,500 separate parts of vocal church music. Long runs of music journals, including the *Musical Times*, *Proceedings of the Royal Musical Association*, *Musical Quarterly*, *Music and*

Letters, and *Revue Grégorienne*. Complete files of the *Journal of the American Musicological Society* and *Musica Disciplina* are held. Loans are made to other libraries by special arrangement. Some details of the library were printed as an appendix to the Catalogue of the Plainsong and Medieval Music Society's Library, 1928, p. 33.

CAMBRIDGE: Caius College. Famous for its large 16th-century mss volumes of masses and motets. There are several autographs of Charles Wood, Professor of Music from 1924–1926.

CAMBRIDGE: Clare College. Has the original mss of Cecil Sharp's folk-song collections and a small collection of early English organ music from the library of Dr T. H. Coles.

CAMBRIDGE: Corpus Christi College. Contains the unique ms of Walter de Odington's *De Speculationae musices*: a 10th-century ms containing two treatises by Hucbald and the *Enchiridion* of Odo of Cluny; and the famous *Winchester Troper*. A printed catalogue of the mss in the library was compiled by Dr M. R. James in 1912.

CAMBRIDGE: Fitzwilliam Museum. One of the most important collections in England. The Museum was founded in 1816 by the will of Richard, 7th Viscount Fitzwilliam of Merrion, who bequeathed his collections of works of art, including autograph ms and printed music, to the University of Cambridge. Rarities include the Fitzwilliam Virginal Book; Compositions by John Bull, John Blow and Purcell; 67 Volumes of J. C. Smith's ms copies of Handel's works; and several autographs of Bach, Beethoven, Bliss, Brahms, J. F. Bridge, Busoni, Chopin, G. F. Macfarren, Moscheles, Mozart, Scarlatti, Schubert, Wagner, Weber, and Samuel Wesley. The mss include operas, cantatas, madrigals, songs and religious music by English, French and Italian composers of the 16th–18th centuries and some instrumental music of the 18th century. There are rare motets of Lalande and scarce harpsichord music of the 17th–18th centuries. A catalogue of the music in the library was compiled by J. A. Fuller Maitland and A. H. Mann in 1893 and a revision is in preparation.

CAMBRIDGE: King's College. Rowe Music Library. 1,000 volumes of music literature, over 10,000 scores, 2,014 miniature scores, 258 full scores, and 1,132 records including all the Argo Shakespeare. The collection is primarily for the use of members of King's but other persons may receive permission on application to the Librarian.

The Rowe Music Library is almost exclusively the gift of one devoted, anonymous member of the college who began his long list of benefactions in 1928 with the library of his friend, Louis Thompson Rowe. Rowe was born in 1855, the eldest of three sons of a grocer, and spent his whole life as a conveyancing clerk in London. He was also a good pianist, an expert linguist, a member of the Oxford and Cambridge Musical Club, and a member of the Bibliographical Society. He was killed in a road accident in 1927. Since his death, his collection has received important additions, including the collected works of 25 great composers; modern reprints of old music and over 1,100 miniature scores.

In 1930, the library acquired over 500 items from the music library of the late Dr A. H. Mann, organist of King's from 1876–1929. Here are 42 early editions of Handel, 85 Handel libretti, early theoretical works and 18th-century song-books.

There are the 3 Denkmäler series, *L'Arte Musicale in Italia*, *Bibliotheca di rarita musicale* and *Classici della musica Italiana;* The English Madrigal School; The English School of Lutenist Song-writers; Tudor Church Music, and foreign collections of Spain, France and Belgium. Opera, oratorio and choral music are represented by over 800 full or vocal operatic scores including 2 Lully full scores *Amadis* (1684) and *Armide* (1686); 42 Handel; 93 full scores of French operas of the late 18th and early 19th centuries; all but one of the Verdi operas in vocal score and all the major Wagner operas. There is a contemporary ms of Scarlatti's *La Ginditta* in a fine binding and Purcell's *Te Deum and Jubilate for St Cecilia's Day 1694*.

There are about 70 late 18th- and early 19-century concertos in parts, many of them in contemporary ms and some extremely interesting 17th-century mss of chamber music, given by the late Lord Keynes. The large pianoforte repertoire has most of the usual and much of the unusual in it. Not least, D. Scarlatti's *Essercizi per Gravicembalo* engraved by Benjamin Fortier, adjudged the most beautiful book in the library. A curious scroll dated 1580 contains 57 rounds and catches, and theoretical works span the period from 1547 on. There is the only known complete copy of Walsh and Hare's *The Bird Fancyer's Delight c.* 1730 and a large number of Walsh arrangements. A more detailed account by Jill Vlasto can be found in *The Music Review*, vol. XII, No. 1, February 1951.

CAMBRIDGE: Magdalene College. The Pepysian Library contains

a few early works on music by Butler, Holder, Morelli, Victorini, Wallis and Alstedius; valuable ms collections of vocal music of the time of Edward IV, Henry VII and Henry VIII (English, French, Scottish and Latin psalters), compositions by Blome, de Bacilly, Kircher, Merseune, Morley, Salmon, Dering, Marbeck, Coperario, Lawes, King, Purcell and Finger; ballads, songs and other compositions adjusted to the compass of Pepys's voice. A ms of special importance is the *Remède d'amour* by G. de Marchant, containing musical settings of several of the lyrics.

CAMBRIDGE: Peterhouse College. Ms anthems, services, masses and motets in Latin and English in four separate part-books, which date from the early part of the 16th century. Over eighty different composers are represented together with many anonymous compositions. An up-to-date catalogue was compiled by Dom Anselm Hughes and issued in 1955.

CAMBRIDGE: Trinity College. Items include Wilson's *Psalterium Carolinum* 1657, and his *Cheerful Ayres* 1660; Locke's *Present Practice of Music Vindicated* 1673; Carr's *Vinculum Societatis* 1687; four volumes of Zarlino's Works 1589; and early editions of works by the Tudor and Stuart composers. Among the mss is the most valuable 15th-century roll of English carols, which was published by J. A. Fuller Maitland and W. S. Rockstro in 1891. Other mss of interest are the collection of lute music in tablature by R. Taylor, R. Johnson, D. Bacheler and T. Greaves; a volume of *Ayres to be sung to ye lute and basse vyole* by G. Handford 1609; the medius of some anthems by G. Loosemore 1664 and two 15th-century Greek mss with music. Dr M. R. James compiled a catalogue of western manuscripts in the Library of Trinity College, Cambridge, in 1901–1904.

CAMBRIDGE: University Library. Benefits under the copyright act and has mss of great rarity from the 13th century onwards. A remarkable collection of 16th-century lute and lyre-viol tablatures also, in which John Dowland and Alfonso Ferrabosco are represented among many others. Early printed music includes rare part-books of works by Thomas Morley, John Ward, Thomas Weelkes, John Wilbye and Nicholas Yonge. The F. T. Arnold bequest received in 1944 has 17th- and 18th-century compositions, and there are first editions of Bach, Handel, Arne, Beethoven and Brahms. There is also an extensive collection of modern English scores.

CANTERBURY: Cathedral Library. Approximately 525 items. Has a ms set of chants from the 13th to 17th centuries and a defective copy of the contratenor cantoris of the rare Barnard's *Church Music* 1641. The library suffered badly as a result of bombing in the 1939–45 War.

DUBLIN: National Library of Ireland. The general collection has 2,250 volumes of music literature and 12,000 scores. Special collections include songs and dance music of the 18th and 19th centuries. Dr Jasper Joly's collection of 23,500 volumes and pamphlets has 683 volumes of Irish and Scottish Song books. Virtually every item is now scarce and many of the items are not to be found in other copyright libraries. The incomplete book of tunes composed by Carolan the harper (1670–1738), published about 1720 by John and William Neal of Christchurch Yard, Dublin, is the only copy known.

Photostatic copies of 870 airs collected by Dr Henry Hudson, musical editor of the *Citizen or Dublin Monthly Magazine* are in the Library. A large collection of printed and manuscript scores together with books on music, were presented by George Noble, Count Plunkett in 1942. There are 400 volumes which were the property of Anglo-Irish families whose names are embossed on the covers. These show the level of musical accompaniment attained by the aristocracy in the 18th and 19th centuries.

The Irish collection has all early editions of Moore's Melodies; Hibernian Catch Club publications; Playford's *Musical Companion*; and O'Farrell's *Music for the Irish Pipes*. Photocopying services are available.

DUBLIN: Royal Irish Academy of Music – Monteagle Memorial Library. Has 200 volumes of music literature and 10,250 scores. Special collections include Bach's Gesellschaft; the Ancient Concert Society of Dublin and the Stanford Collection.

DUBLIN: Trinity College. A copyright library, containing the Ebenezer Prout collection and some 16th–18th-century music, including the lute books of W. Ballet and T. Dallis. A catalogue of the mss in the library was compiled by T. K. Abbott in 1900.

DURHAM: Cathedral Library. Specializes in early music, both printed and manuscript, as may be expected, from the medieval period to the 17th century. Special collections include the Falle collection of 17th-century music, mostly printed in Holland; the

Bamburgh collection of early printed and ms music; 17th-century part books. Books and like material are not lent, but microfilm is supplied to personal researchers in many parts of the world.

EDINBURGH: National Library of Scotland. A copyright library, with 5,000 volumes of music literature and 145,000 scores. The main music catalogue is on cards in order of composer, compiled according to British Museum rules. Special collections include:

(a) The John Glen Collection of Scottish music and musical literature, with 412 volumes containing over 900 items. See John Glen's *Early Scottish Melodies*, 1900.

(b) The Alexander Wood Inglis collection of English and Scottish music of the 18th and early 19th centuries in 306 volumes containing 740 items.

(c) The William Cowan collection of over 1,000 liturgical works, including psalters and hymns from the 16th to the 20th century.

(d) The Balfour Handel collection of about 650 items, mostly early editions of Handel's works with some foreign editions and over 100 libretti which was formed by Julian Marshall, bought from him by A. J. Balfour and eventually purchased by the Library.

(e) The Hopkinson Berlioz collection of 325 music items plus books, mss and autograph letters, scenic designs, posters and portraits concerned with Hector Berlioz and presented in 1952 by Cecil Hopkinson.

(f) Manuscript scores, some autographed, of works by Percy Grainger presented by his widow in 1962.

Its chief treasures are the Skene mss and the Scone Antiphonarium (Carver mss) dating from the early 16th century which contain much sacred music composed by Robert Carver.

EDINBURGH: Reid Music Library, the University. Is the Library of the Faculty of Music. Has 6,500 volumes of music literature, 24,000 scores, 3,000 miniature scores, 21,000 full scores and 4,750 gramophone records. The mss include a 15th-century psalter with neumes: some oratorios by Hasse: and an orchestral suite by Telemann. The last four professors of music – Oakley, Donaldson,

Niecks and Tovey – made large additions to the library. The Professor F. Weiss collection comprises books on Beethoven.

The general library of the University has the Dunkeld Music, Book, 16th century; a Scots Metrical Psalter compiled by Thomas Wood 1562–78; Sir William Mure's Lute Book *c*. 1600–1650; Mure's Music Book early 17th century; and various 17th-century songs.

Dr Hans Gals compiled the *Catalogue of Mss, Printed Books and Books on Music to 1850* in the Library of the Music Department of the University of Edinburgh, Reid Library, issued in 1941 but this does not include the Sir Donald Tovey and Professor Weiss collections.

ETON COLLEGE: Rackley Music Library. 350 volumes of musical literature: 730 miniature scores: 225 full scores and thousands of musical items plus 1,553 records. The College has 25 pianos and special collections include the Bach Gesellschaft; the Purcell Society and Boyce's Cathedral Music. The arrangement of the large collection of music is alphabetical by composer.

GLASGOW: University Library. Has many special collections including:

(*a*) The Y. L. Stillie collection of 760 volumes including many full scores and operatic works.

(*b*) The W. Eving collection of 2,500 books on music, 2,500 volumes of music and 95 mss. Here are seven examples of Gaffurio from 1480; Burtin's 1487; the *Flores Musice* 1488; a Boethius of 1492; early editions of Byrd's Psalms; 47 volumes of Praetorius and an extensive collection of English psalters and hymn books. An anonymous catalogue was published in 1878 and a new and more comprehensive edition is in preparation.

(*c*) The L. Zavertal collection of 94 volumes of music, autographs of composers and Mozart relics described in *New Mozartiana* by H. G. Farmer and H. Smith, 1935.

(*d*) The collection of modern Scottish composers of 511 volumes, with works by Drysdale, Lamond, MacGunn, McEwen, Moffat, Moonie and Roberton.

(*e*) The Scottish Music Collection of 424 volumes originally formed by H. G. Farmer which is particularly rich in reels, strathspeys, and national songs.

(*f*) The Farmer collection of 720 books on music and 317 scores including 40 mss mainly relating to oriental music. The works of almost every famous Arabic, Turkish and Persian writer on the theory of music are here.

GLOUCESTER: Cathedral Library. Houses a small collection including incomplete choir books, a mss full score of Boyce's *Blessed is He*, some illuminated mss and some printed and ms church music of the 17th century.

HEREFORD: Cathedral: the Chain Library. Predominantly theological. Has glees, songs and pianoforte music which belonged to Fanny Kemble; two sets of *organ concertos* by W. Felton and Kircher's *Musurgia* 1650. There are anthems, services and other church music of the 18th and 19th centuries, some in manuscript, about 325 items in all.

LEEDS: University: Brotherton Library. 3,600 volumes of music literature, 9,000 scores, 2,000 miniature scores, 7,000 full scores and 670 gramophone records. Gafori's *Practica musicae* 1497 and Kircher's *Musurgia* 1650 are rare possessions. A collection of 70 letters from Mendelssohn to Moscheles. Publications include a Handlist of the Novello-Cowden Clarke collection, 1955 and a catalogue of the Romany collection, 1962. Additions to the Novello-Cowden Clarke Collection include ms diaries of V. and M. Novello for the Mozart pilgrimage to Austria with other diaries and letters.

LINCOLN: Cathedral Library. Printed editions of Byrd's *Sacred Songs, Psalms and Sonnets* in 5 quarto volumes, 1588, and John Dowland's *Songs and Ayres with tablature for the lute*, 3 volumes – 1600, 1613 and 1642. These, and a few other mss, are described in R. W. Woolley's *Catalogue of the MSS of Lincoln Cathedral Chapter Library* 1927.

LONDON: American Library. 5,500 scores and 6,000 records which may be borrowed by anyone resident in Great Britain. Catalogues have been issued covering *Scores and printed music; Recordings of music by Americans; Recordings of popular and folk music from America; Books on music in the United States.* (This Library specializes in American music only.)

LONDON: B.B.C. Music Library. The B.B.C. Music Library at

Yalding House, 152 Great Portland Street, London, W.1 exists to organize the supply of music for broadcasts throughout the whole of the Corporation and has probably the most extensive collection in existence, of music for performance. Its reference library houses most of the collected editions, a complete set of the Hofmeister catalogues, a comprehensive array of modern thematic and publishers' catalogues, with a wide range of music library catalogues and bibliographies. There are thousands of orchestral scores and parts, many of which contain detailed timings and conductors' markings, and duplicate sets are seconded to the various regional stations, which also have extensive libraries. A unique and valuable sequence of over 30,000 sets of manuscript scores and parts consists of specially commissioned music incidental to broadcast plays and features. The libraries of Percy Pitt, Sir Landon Ronald, Sir Adrian Boult, Eldridge Newman, Percy Cross, A. H. Fox Strangways and Frederick Bonavia have been purchased in whole or part. Vocal scores and part songs account for over a quarter of a million items. These range from bulk quantities for the large choral bodies, to single rare scores. A Choral Reference Library and an Opera Reference Library of master scores, timed and often cued, are other unique holdings. Songs are catalogued by composer and title, and the libretti collection includes many commissioned scripts for broadcasting. The chamber music collection has many manuscript works and the B.B.C. employs its own highly skilled copiers for the preservation, restoration and duplication of scores, which can be reproduced by the die-line process. A staff of 55 administers the library, the chief divisions of which are Requisitions, Hiring and copying, Shelf issues and maintenance, and Accessions – divided into orchestral, choral, songs and chamber music.

Excellent catalogues on the loose-leaf principle have been compiled of these voluminous collections and their value cannot be estimated. These are used internally in the Corporation but a set has been deposited with the Central Library at Westminster. Lists of new accessions are issued from time to time which are circulated widely at home and abroad. The library is confined to use for broadcasts and as may well be imagined, programmes are scheduled months in advance in order to give the librarian time to procure the music required. An out-of-print report will not do for the B.B.C. Even if only a single copy of a work is extant, it must be obtained if required, no matter at what expense or distance.

LONDON: British Museum. Has one of the richest collections of music and musical literature in the world estimated at 1¼ million pieces, which falls into four parts:

(1) The collection of mss and printed music within the Department of Printed Books.
(2) The Royal Music Library.
(3) The mss collections of the Royal College of Music.
(4) The Library of the Royal Philharmonic Society.
The last three are on loan.

(1) The mss number over 3,000 volumes and include the Thomas Mulliner book of 16th-century music: autographs of all the famous composers from Purcell onwards; the Chapel Royal mss and the Tregian mss of madrigals and fancies for strings. Catalogues have been compiled:

(a) *Catalogue of Additions to the mss in the British Museum.* 1854–1860.
(b) A Hughes-Hughes. *A catalogue of manuscript music in the British Museum.* 1906–1909. 3 vols.

The printed music consists in the main of deposits from 1790 onwards under the terms of the Copyright Acts. Published catalogues are:

(a) The accessions of modern music from 1884 to date.
(b) W. Barclay Squire. *Catalogue of Printed Music published between 1487 and 1800* . . . 1912. 1st supplement 1912: 2nd supplement 1940: 3rd supplement in preparation.
(c) K. Meyer and P. Hirsch. *Katalog der Bibliothek Paul Hirsch*, 1928–1947. 4 vols.
(d) A. Hyatt King and C. Humphries. *Catalogue of Printed Music in the British Museum :* Accessions pt. 53 – music in the Hirsch Library, 1951.

(2) The Royal Music Library.
    The property of H.M. the Queen, but has been on permanent loan since 1911. The collection was formed by George III, greatly increased by George IV, and added to by Queen Victoria and Prince Albert. This remarkably rich collection is renowned for its Handel Collection, which includes mss and fine bindings. A catalogue was published in 3 vols. in

1927–1929 compiled by W. Barclay Squire and H. Andrews – *Catalogue of the King's Music Library.*

(3) The Royal College of Music Mss Collection has been on loan since 1954. There are thousands of items, and among them, autographs by Haydn, Mozart, Schubert and others.

(4) The Royal Philharmonic Society's Library dates from 1813 and most of the works deposited on loan are autographs, many of them commissioned by the Society.

Obviously, only a brief account can be given of the vast amount of valuable and rare material in the British Museum. There is a much fuller description in Grove's *Dictionary* and also in the Proceedings of the Royal Musical Association 1952–3 which feature an article by the keeper in charge of the collections of Printed Music, A. Hyatt King, on *The Music Room of the British Museum 1753–1953: its history and organization.*

LONDON: Gresham College Library. Both printed and ms material. The 321 volumes of printed works include Arne, Attwood, Bach, Boyce, Eccles, Fremart (8 masses published in Paris 1624–1645), Galuppi, Handel, Horsley, Mozart, Paisiello, Playford, Purcell, Sarti, Stevens and Walmisley. The ms material, in 124 volumes, is being catalogued and here are works by Blow, Handel, Jomelli and Purcell.

LONDON: Royal Academy of Music. 5,000 volumes of music literature, 60,000 scores, 2,000 miniature scores, 5,000 full scores and 400 records for the use of lecturers. Formed in 1823 from many fine collections, including the music library of the founder, John Fane, Lord Burghersh, 11th Earl of Westmorland; George IV's donation of the Arnold edition of Handel in 1825; the libraries of R. J. S. Stevens and the English Bach Society. Special collections include the Henry Wood Library of 3,000 scores and parts; the Angelina Goetz library of opera and ballet; the G. D. Cunningham library of organ music; and many manuscripts and autographs. A printed catalogue of the Goetz Library was issued in 1903 and ms catalogues have been made of the Sir Henry Wood Library and the printed orchestral scores of the Royal Philharmonic Society.

LONDON: Royal College of Music. One of the richest and most extensive collections in the United Kingdom. Founded in 1883, the Library was built up by a series of important gifts and bequests, including the libraries of the Sacred Harmonic Society; the Concerts of Antient Music presented by Queen Victoria; Sir George Grove; the Musical Union and others. The Library is in three parts: (1) a reference library containing all rare editions, works of historical and critical interest; (2) a comprehensive collection of complete editions; (3) a large working library of general musical literature. The mss of the College are deposited on loan in the British Museum, whilst the Heron collection of books on the violin and the Sandford Terry Bach collection are deposited in the Faculty of Music Library at Oxford University. W. Barclay Squire compiled a *Catalogue of Printed Music in the Library of the Royal College of Music, London* in 1909.

LONDON: University: Music Library. Has 6,500 volumes of music literature, 10,000 scores including full scores, 1,600 miniature scores and 5,000 gramophone records. The Music Library was opened in 1926 and has some of the outstanding theoretical works of the 15th, 16th and 17th centuries, including Gaffurio, Niger, Marbeck; Day's Psalms 1563 and William Lawes's *Choice Psalms* 1648. Special collections on permanent loan include the libraries of Sir George Elvey, the Royal Musical Association, the Plainsong and Medieval Music Society built up since the 1890s and including all the liturgical and music books formerly belonging to Rev. Thomas Helmore and the Oxford and Cambridge Musical Club.

Some 20,000 photostat reproductions of Tudor Church music are also held. Equipment includes a Dynatron Stereo record player; a Leak player and a Steck Pianola grand.

LONDON: Victoria and Albert Museum. 375 volumes of music literature and autographs of Mendelssohn's *Hear my prayer* and Bishop's *Legends of the Rhine*. Only books relevant to the study of musical instruments owned by the Museum are acquired. Occasional music lectures are given and there is a regular series of Sunday evening concerts in the Raphael Cartoon Gallery. Publication No. 40, *Early Keyboard Instruments* in the *Small Picture Books Series* illustrates specimens in the Department of Woodwork.

MANCHESTER: John Rylands Library. Has valuable music mss dating from the 9th century and its printed books include Marbeck's *Booke of Common Praier . . . 1550* and Sternhold and Hopkins *Psalter* 1562.

MANCHESTER: Royal College of Music. 1,000 volumes of music literature, 10,000 scores and 630 gramophone records. Equipment includes a Chapman radiogram and speaker, and a Portogram record player. Special collections include historic instruments from Dr Henry Watson and a working collection of modern instruments for loan to students.

OXFORD: Bodleian Library. A copyright library. Has valuable ms material from the 10th century which has been published in catalogue form, *Medieval polyphony in the Bodleian Library* by Dom Anselm Hughes, 1951. Sir John Stainer and Sir Sidney Nicholson listed the important examples of medieval music in their *Early Bodleian music* whilst W. H. Frere's *Bibliotheca musico-liturgica* deals with liturgical mss with music. *The Summary Catalogues of Western MSS*, vols. 4 and 5 describe the music held of the 16th, 17th and 18th centuries. In 1947 a complete collection of Handel's published instrumental music was received, the Bourne collection. A fuller account of the Bodleian collections is given in Grove's *Dictionary*.

OXFORD: Christ Church. 8,000 items mainly of early English and foreign music. The 10 volumes of Barnard's *Church Music* were acquired from Hereford Cathedral Library in 1918. Catalogues of the mss by G. E. P. Arkwright were published in 1915 and 1923.[1] A catalogue of the printed music by A. Hiff was published in 1919 and a thematic catalogue of the anonymous instrumental music is available in the library in two volumes.

OXFORD: Faculty of Music Library. Over 13,000 items, including 1,806 miniature scores, 600 full scores and 2,000 collected editions. Bound periodicals number almost 600 and there are 300 records for the use of lecturers. Equipment includes a Bush player, a Pye table model and a Ginn console. There are eight pianos, two Bechstein uprights and Bechstein, Blüthner and Rogers grands. Two permanent loan collections consist of the Heron-Allen collection of books on the violin and the Sandford Terry Bach collection, deposited by the Royal College of Music. In addition, there is a sizeable collection of English printed music of the late 17th, 18th and 19th centuries.

TENBURY: St Michael's College. The most important private library of antiquarian music and musical literature in the United Kingdom, with a large number of early mss, especially of the Tudor

[1] Volume 3 was never published.

5

period. Here is Handel's Conductor's score of the *Messiah* used in Dublin at the first performance in 1742. Other interesting items are ms scores of operas, some from the royal music library of the French kings, and a set of service books from the French royal chapel. A catalogue of the mss was edited by Dr E. H. Fellowes in 1934, and a fuller account is given in Grove's *Dictionary*.

WORCESTER: Cathedral Library. About 1,000 items, including a Benedictine antiphoner of the 13th century written at Worcester Cathedral; a Hereford Missal of the 14th century; some parts of Barnard's *Church Music* and a quantity of flyleaves of harmonized music of the period 1275–1325. These, along with others at the Bodleian, the British Museum and Magdalen College, Oxford, total about 110 items which have been transcribed and edited by Dom Anselm Hughes in his *Worcester medieval harmony of the 13th and 14th centuries*, 1928, and have been described in the Proceedings of the Royal Musical Association for 1924–5.

YORK MINSTER: Music Library. 300 printed scores especially of the 17th century, 150 mss and a few volumes of music literature. It is essentially an antiquarian and historical collection and among the rarer items may be mentioned an Installation Ode by Hague; The Nativity by Homilius; a mass by Naumann; a four-part book of fantasies by Jenkins, Ward and Tomkins; 8 choirbooks containing voice parts of 17th-century anthems and services; autograph mss of the works of Walmisley and Stanford; 13 motets by Carissimi; 2 valuable part-books containing services by Byrd, Parsons and others, one of which, the Dunnington-Jefferson ms is described in the Appendix to Tudor Church Music; 12 concerti by Albinoni. A detailed account of the Library appeared in the *Musical Times* for February 1958.

9

Overseas Libraries

AUSTRALIA

BRISBANE, Queensland Public Library. 1,169 volumes of music literature, 69 scores, 37 miniature and 32 full scores.

MELBOURNE, State Library of Victoria. 3,620 volumes of music literature, 8,059 scores, 620 miniature and 1,331 full scores. Music published in Victoria is received under copyright. Rare items include a 10th-century manuscript on vellum, *De Musica* by Boethius, which is illustrated with many technically interesting diagrams. The volume also contains an abridgement of *Musica Enchiriades* attributed to Huchbald. There is a French choir book *c.* 1350, a rare example of antiphony from the School of Jean Pucelle; seven leaves from an Italian Antiphoner *c.* 1290; a French manuscript, the *Missale Trajecteuse* made for use in Utrecht in 1497; and a very rare Service Book, the *Hildesheim missal*, Nuremberg, 1499.

Original manuscripts include Mendelssohn's *Songs without words* and Wienawski's *Scherzo Tarantelle*, both autographed; an original manuscript sketch to Schumann's *Fantasia for the violin* dedicated to and containing an inscription in Joachim's writing; and a manuscript written for Dame Nellie Melba by Mme Marchesi.

Special collections are the Dyer collection of works by modern British composers, including some unpublished works of Gustav Holst and the Thomas collection of lieder, art songs and national songs.

The library has a very comprehensive stock with many items of importance and value, as can be seen.

PERTH, Library Board of Western Australia. 2,081 volumes of musical literature, 4,828 scores, 670 miniature scores, 125 full scores, 55 records and 44 periodicals. The Music Library is in the process of being established by the Library Board and the Music

Council of Western Australia Inc. It opened in 1963 and will be the first state music lending library in Australia Present holdings include Gesellschaft editions of 16 major composers; the *Musica Disciplina* and *Musicological Studies and documents* series published by the American Institute of Musicology. Classification of music scores is according to the British Catalogue of Music Scheme and an Information Circular is issued every 3 to 4 months.

SYDNEY, City Library. 3,216 volumes of music literature and 665 scores. A printed catalogue, *The Literature of music*, was published in 1949.

SYDNEY, Public Library of New South Wales. This library comprises several departments, the principal ones being the General Reference Department and the Mitchell Library. The latter is a special research collection for Australasia and the South Pacific.

The General Reference Department has 3,000 volumes of music literature and 5,000 scores. A duplicated typescript catalogue was issued in 1921 and has supplements from 1922–24: from 1925–31 (A – Harmony) and from 1934, on cards.

The Mitchell Library has 1,000 volumes of musical literature, 4,000 scores and 70 records. All New South Wales publications are acquired under copyright deposit and the Australian context is interpreted in its widest sense. Here, therefore, you will find music by non-Australians with words by Australians, and music by non-Australians but with an Australian interest. Most music scores are filed vertically under the names of the composers and entries for all musical items are included in the general catalogue. A supplementary music catalogue, on cards, was maintained until 1942.

TASMANIA: State Library. 2,500 volumes of music literature, 1,000 scores, 312 miniature scores, 700 full scores and 5,800 records.

AUSTRIA

AUGSBURG, Staats und Stadtbibliotheks, Schaezlerstrasse, 25. About 2,000 volumes of early printed and ms music chiefly from the suppressed monasteries of the city. There are alphabetical card and classified printed catalogues.

Hans Michael Schletterer compiled a *Katalog der in der Stadtbibliothek, dem ständiger Archive under der Bibliothek des Historischen Vereins zu Augsburg befindlichen*. Musikwerke, Berlin 1878. Special collections include over 1,000 hymnals of Hans M. Schletterer and 249 letters from the music collection of the Augsburg Kapellmeister, Carl Ludwig Drobisch.

SALZBURG, Bibliotek der Internationale Stiffung Mozarteum. A unique library containing practically all the literature relating to Mozart. There are 1,400 books; 30,000 scores; 500 miniature scores and 50 gramophone records. It possesses original family letters and fragments of scores. Publications include: New *Mozart ausgabe* and *Mozart Yearbook* since 1950.

BELGIUM

BRUSSELS, Bibliothèque royale de Belgique. The library has several sections calling themselves La Réserve précieuse, les Manuscrits and les Imprimés. The rarities include the F. J. Félis collection of 400 works printed before 1700, including works of Roland de Lassus. A catalogue of this collection is in preparation. Amongst the mss are many from the Fétis collection and 2,000 works from the libraries of the Dukes of Burgundy and monasteries of the Low Countries. The printed music covers works and literature of the 18th–20th centuries. There is no separate music department.

BRUSSELS, Bibliothèque du Conservatoire royale de musique. 300,000 musical items of all kinds and 79 periodicals. A catalogue was published in 4 vols. in the period 1898–1912. Special collections include:

(1) Westphal of C. P. E. Bach and G. Telemann.
(2) Sainte-Gudule, especially of the 18th century.
(3) Hollenfeltz of Mozart and his family.
(4) Part of the Wagner collection.
(5) 6,000 libretti.

CZECHOSLOVAKIA

PRAGUE, Municipal Public Library: Smetana Music Library. 10,000 volumes of music literature, 175,000 scores, 3,000 miniature scores, 2,500 full scores and 2,500 records. 12 bibliographies have been published of Czech composers, including Václav Dobiáš, Jan Seidel and Antonín Dvořák. Special collections include Gesellschafts of various composers, and old prints. A recent bibliography covers the gramophone record literature of the dance.

PRAGUE, State Library of the Socialist Republic. 25,000 volumes of music literature; 65,000 scores; 1,200 miniature and 4,000 full scores, plus 573 records. Has mss ranging from the 12th to 15th centuries; music mss for the 16th to 20th centuries; and old prints.

DENMARK

COPENHAGEN. Kommunes biblioteker (Hoved biblioteket. Musikaf delingen). 3,000 volumes of music literature: 8,000 scores: 500 miniature and 250 full scores. There are both card and printed catalogues in four parts covering orchestral and chamber music; piano and organ; vocal music; dramatic music.

COPENHAGEN. Det Kongelige Danske Musikkonservatorium's Bibliotek, Copenhagen. 1,500 vols. of musical literature; 25,000 scores, 1,100 miniature scores and 500 full scores, plus 1,000 records. Has the Niels W. Gade and J. P. E. Hartmann collections.

FLENSBORG. Dansk Central bibliotek for Sydslesvig. 160 vols. of music literature, 747 scores and 280 gramophone records.

FREDERIKSBERG Public Libraries. No special music department. Music literature is included in the art and biography sections, and in addition, there are 3,939 scores and 603 miniature scores.

FINLAND

HELSINKI, Sibelius – Akatemian Kirjasto. 34,500 volumes of music literature; 30,300 scores; 1,300 miniature scores; 700 full scores and 1,300 gramophone records. Has Beam Echo and Collaro equipment and a Hellas piano. Houses the Music Library of Evert Katila which is in the possession of the Musicians' Federation of Finland, containing about 1,600 volumes.

FRANCE

LYON, Bibliothèque de la ville. 5,000 volumes of musical literature, 1,600 scores, 400 miniature scores and 500 full scores. This musical collection contains items from the *Académie du Concert* founded at Lyon in 1713 by the composer Nicolas Bergiron du fort Michon and the physician J. P. Christin, famous for his work on the thermometer. Difficult financial obligations disappeared by 1772 and nine years earlier, the child Mozart had given a concert at the Académie on the clavichord. The library was made complete in 1894 by the acquiring of the Becker collection at Nancy, consisting of about 700 scores, both ms and printed, of French and Italian composers of the 17th and 18th centuries which the academicians had received in Paris or Rome, or who had composed at Lyon. Amongst the rarities is an unknown Scarlatti oratorio *Il mastirio di santa Orsola* which was discovered and identified by Ennemond Trillat, director of the conservatoire at Lyon.

PARIS, Bibliothèque Nationale : Bibliothèque du Conservatoire de Musique. Very full information is given in Grove which is considered by the library authorities to be overdone. As is to be expected, the collection is enormous : 40,000 volumes of music literature, 700,000 scores and 2,500 miniature scores. A catalogue was compiled in 1885 by J. B. Weckerlin *Bibliothèque du Conservatoire national de musique . . . Catalogue bibliographique des principaux ouvrages de la Réserve*. Special features include 20,000 manuscripts ; 50,000 autograph letters ; La Musique collection du Roi ; La musique des Menus plaisirs, des collections particulières ; all copyright French music since 1835 ; collections of prints and newspaper cuttings ; all the mss of the Concours d'Essais and most of those of the Concours de Rome.

PARIS, Marc Pincherle, 132 Boulevard Exelmans, Paris XVIᵉ. This is a private library and consists of approximately 5,000 volumes of music literature and 2,000 scores. There are many autograph letters which have been published by the owner in his *Musiciens peints par eux-mêmes*, Paris, 1939.

STRASBOURG, Bibliothèque de l'Institut de Musicologie de l'Université de Strasbourg. 5,000 volumes of music literature ; 3,000 scores ; 200 miniature scores and 500 full scores. The University collections are used for teaching and research.

VERSAILLES, Bibliothèque municipale classée, 5 rue de l'Indépendance-Americaine, Versailles. There are 1,500 volumes of music literature in Augusta Holmes' collection and other volumes on ancient music. In addition 1,500 scores of the 17th and 18th centuries and 650 not yet catalogued of the 19th century, again from the Holmes collection, plus 107 gramophone records. A *Catalogue méthodique* was compiled in 1845 by M. Le Roi, and in 1888, a printed catalogue of manuscripts, by Mm. Delerot and Taphanel. Of the mss there are 35 copies of the works of Philidor; 37 of Lully; 16 of Lalande; 9 of Moreau; 25 of Boely, and the works of Clérambault, Couperin, Marchand, Rameau and many others. In the general collection of manuscripts are Metoyen's beautiful watercolours consisting of *Plans, Coupes et Elévations des Tribunes et Orchestres de la Musique de Roi* à Versailles, Compiègne, Fontainebleau et Choisy. The Society of Friends of the Library organizes concerts in the Louis XV gallery.

GERMANY

ASCHAFFENBURG, Städt musikschule bibliotheque est. 1905. 509 volumes of music literature and 6,017 scores.

AUGSBURG, Städt musikbücherei, est. 1958. 1,052 volumes of music literature, 2,387 scores, 84 records, 1 tape recorder and 1 record player, 2 listening rooms, 1 lecture room and an exhibition room.

BERLIN, Amerika – Gedenkbibliothek/Berliner Zentralbibliothek Blücherplatz, Berlin, 61. 3,405 volumes of music literature: 12,245 scores, 1,423 miniature scores, 936 full scores and 3,908 records for playing in the library only. Has 3 pianos, 1 harpsichord, 7 record players, 1 tape recorder, 2 Hi-Fi installations and 1 stereophonic installation. Accommodation includes an auditorium, a conference room, a music room and three listening booths which will hold four persons each and are sound-proof. Musical programmes are given in the evenings including complete operas and oratorios; symphonic and chamber music; folklore, with tapes and records; poetry and drama. Various ensembles give recitals of chamber music and jazz; lectures and exhibitions are staged and the library acts as a focal point for amateur musicians. The collections include complete editions of J. S. Bach, Buxtehude and Scheidt, and the complete works of Bartók, Hindemith, Schönberg, Richard Strauss and Stravinsky. There are 120 scores of the Vivaldi complete edition and other collections include Notenarchiv symphonies, overtures, concertos; *Denkmäler deutscher Tonkunst; Nagels Musikarchiv; Hortus musicus*. Music for chamber orchestra of the baroque and pre-German classic periods. There is an author index of songs, records for learning foreign languages and records of the folklore of all five continents.

BERLIN, Charlottenberg, Städt Musikbücherei, est. 1935. 2,174 volumes of music literature, 7,961 scores, 1,200 records, 1 record player and 1 listening room.

BERLIN, Deutsche musik – Phonothek est. 1961. Has 350 volumes of music literature and 10,300 records. Listening studios. This recently established institute collects all the records produced in Western Germany.

BERLIN, Deutsche Staatsbibliothek, 330,000 textbooks and scores, 195 periodicals and 6,700 records; one of the foremost collections in the world. Celebrated its third centenary in 1961, an occasion marked by the publication of (a) a detailed history and future assessment of the State Library with a fine illustrated account of the music department by Karl Heinz Köhler, the present director; and (b) a life and bibliography of Carl Maria Von Weber. The library has the complete works of J. S. Bach, Mozart, Beethoven, Cherubini, Mendelssohn, Weber, Schumann, Nicolai, Busoni and many others.

BERLIN, Institut für Musikforschung. 10,200 volumes of music literature, 1,850 scores, 180 miniature scores, 25 full scores and 650 gramophone records. 40 periodicals are taken. Special collections and features include: a collection of musical instruments, in the Berlin Public Museum; illustrations and photographs of musical history; 3,000 autographs comprising the Meyerbeer archives; a small collection of autograph letters of composers. Publications include *Musikinstrumentenkunde*, a catalogue of museum holdings, music publishers' publications, and special notices in books, periodicals and newspapers.

The former library of the Städtliches Institut was lost in the War and a new beginning was made in 1947.

BERLIN, Neukölln, Musikbücherei est. 1948. 1,611 volumes of music literature, 8,558 scores, 1 tape recorder, 1 record player.

BERLIN, Phonogramm-Archiv des Museums für Völkerkunde. Has 556 volumes of music literature and 508 records containing 1,929 compositions. The Berlin Phonogramm-Archiv was founded in 1900 with the object of preserving, in the interests of research and scholarship, original aufnahmen aussereuropäischer. At present, it has 2,060 pieces on 1,665 phonographic rolls, and 8,639 original pieces on tape.

BERLIN, Steglitz Städt Musikbücherei, est. 1928. 2,924 volumes of music literature, 9,919 scores, 1 record player, 1 tape recorder. Arranges concerts and record evenings.

BIELEFELD, Musikbücherei, est. 1941. 2,525 volumes of music literature, 3,999 scores. Has records and record player, 2 listening studios and record evenings.

BOCHUM, Musikbücherei est. 1925. 2,431 volumes of music literature, 10,459 scores, 1,030 records, 3 record players, 2 tape recorders and 1 piano. Has 3 music studios and arranges record and chamber music evenings. 15 periodicals. 1 lecture room.

DARMSTADT, Hess, Landes- und Hochschulbibliothek. The library suffered heavily during the War and today has 800,000 volumes in all, with but 3,500 musical items including numerous mss of the 18th century. A printed catalogue exists of the original collection: *Die Musikalien der Grossherzoglichen Hofbibliothek in Darmstadt 1874.* A new catalogue is in preparation.

DONAUESCHINGEN, the Library of Prince Fürstenberg. Hofbibliothek. 748 volumes of musical literature, 2,089 music mss and 3,079 musical prints. Special holdings include the works of Mozart and Haydn, but the collection is now closed.

DRESDEN, Sächsische, Landesbibliothek, Musikabteilung. 20,000 scores; 7,962 mss scores and 986 autographs; 5,000 books about music: 2,100 libretti and 950 records. Yearly lists are published of new additions. Special collections include a deposit of church music of the 16th and 17th centuries, both printed and ms editions; collections from the former Royal County School of the 17th and 18th centuries; and operatic archives of the Sächsische State Theatre of the 18th and early 19th centuries. The library is endeavouring to cover lost ground, for during the War, over 46,000 items were destroyed.

DÜSSELDORF, Musikbücherei d. Landeshaubtstadt est. 1923. 1,663 volumes of music literature, 6,052 scores, 833 records, 1 record player, 1 tape recorder. Has lecture evenings and gramophone concerts, 1 listening room and 1 lecture room.

ESSEN, Städt Büchereien, est. 1930. 3,896 volumes of music literature, 13,520 scores, 1,392 records, 5 record players, 1 piano,

11 periodicals. Arranges chamber music evenings. 2 listening studios, 1 music room.

FRANKFURT-AM-MAIN, Städt Folksbüchereien Musikbücherei est. 1928. 2,037 volumes of music literature, 10,113 scores, 624 records, 1 record player, 1 tape recorder, 1 stereo player with two transportable loudspeakers housed in a listening studio. Arranges musical evenings. 13 periodicals.

FRANKFURT-AM-MAIN, Städt-u. Universitäts bibliothek. Musikabteilung. 12,500 volumes of music literature; 15,000 scores and 59 periodicals. Special collections relevant particularly to Frankfurt include:

(a) Choral music of the 17th and 18th centuries.
(b) Collections of choral music from the Frankfurter Church Schools of the 16th and 18th centuries.
(c) Autographs.
(d) Operas.
(e) Portraits.
(f) Theatrical posters.
(g) Concert programmes.
(h) Music mss.

FREIBURG, Niederrheinische, Volksliedarchiv. The essential material of the Archiv consists of about 3,000 folk-songs of the Lower Rhine in their authentic form and 100 folk dances picked up from folk musicians. In addition to the archives, there are scores of symphonic music executed by music societies in the 18th and 19th centuries, and 150 tape recordings.

Publications include:

Schriftenreite des Niederrheinischen Volksliedarchivs, Viersten.

Vol. 1. Klüsen. *Das Volkslied im niederrheinischen Dorf.* Potsdam, 1940.

Vol. 2. Klüsen. *Der Stainmescharakter in den Werken, neuerer deutscher Volkslieder.* Bad Godesberg, 1953.

Praktische Ausgaben
   Die Windmühle, Niederrheinische Volkslieder; ed. Heeren- Klüsen. 1955.
Niederrheinische Volkshände. 1960.

In 1963 they published:

(1) *Des Dülkener Fiedlers Wiederbuch, Neuausgabe mit Melodien.*
(2) *Volkslieder von Niederrheim : ein Bilderbuch.*

GELSENKIRCHEN, Musikbücherei, est. 1961. 1,500 volumes music literature, 2,500 scores, 600 records, 2 record players, 1 tape recorder, 1 listening studio and holds music lectures and opera evenings.

HAMBURG, Musikbücherei, d. Hamburge Offentl. Bücherhalen est. 1915. 8,009 volumes of music literature, 31,964 scores, 1,332 records, 1 record player. Has 1 listening room, 1 music room and arranges concerts, lectures and rehearsals.

HANOVER, Städt bibliotheque/musikapt est. 1940. 2,646 volumes of music literature, 12,395 scores, 806 records, 3 record players, 1 piano. Has 1 listening studio and 6 record cubicles. Stages record recitals.

HEILBRONN, Musikbücherei est. 1961. 465 volumes of music literature, 667 scores, 302 records, 4 record players, 1 tape recorder, 2 listening studios, 1 recording room and 1 lecture room. Has music and record evenings.

KARLSRUHE, Gedische Landsbibliothek. 3,650 volumes of music literature, 3,800 scores including 1,300 manuscripts, 150 miniature scores, 250 full scores and 10 gramophone records. 52 periodicals are taken. 16th-century mss include:

Sebastian VIRDUNG.	*Musica getutscht und ausgezogen.* Besel, 1511.
Hans NEWSIDLER.	*Lutebooks.* Nürmberg 1544.
Sebastian OCHSENKUHN.	*Tabulaturbuch auff die Lanten.* Heydeberg, 1558.
Bernhard JOBIN.	*Lutebooks.* Strassburg, 1572–3.

The theoretical and practical music of the Middle Ages is well represented. Valuable liturgies cover the period from the 9th to the 17th centuries and there are the mss of BERNOS von REICHENAU and the HERMANNUS CONTRACTUS. Most of these came from the monastic libraries of Reichenau, St Georgen, Schwarzach, and especially from St Peter in Schwarzach, which were collected originally by Abbot Jakob Steyrer (1749–1795) from all over the world. (*See* Franz Kern. Ph. J. Steyrer, *in* Freiburger Diozesanarchiv 79.1959.)

New and complete editions of the most famous German musicians have been acquired, including Schütz, Bach, Telemann, Haydn, Mozart, Beethoven, Bruckner, Reger and many others.

Series include: *Denkmäler deutscher Tonkunst.*
Denkmäler der Tonkunst in Osterreich.
Das Erbe deutscher Musik.
Nagels Musikarchiv.

KOBLENZ, Städtbibliotheque/Musikbücherei est. 1955. 1,950 volumes of music literature, 3,800 scores, 620 records, 1 record player, 1 piano. Has 1 listening room with 5 stereo record players and 1 music room where record evenings are held. 18 periodicals.

KÖLN, Musikbücherei est. 1922. 2,152 volumes of music literature, 6,412 scores, 5 record players. Arranges concerts.

KREFELD, Städt Musikbücherei est. 1955. 620 volumes of music literature, 5,080 scores, 320 records, 2 record players and 2 listening studios.

LUDWIGSHAFEN-AM-RHEIN, Städt Musikbücherei est. 1924. 1,575 volumes of music literature and 5,289 scores.

LÜNEBURG, Ratsbücherei/Musikhabt est. 1924. 734 volumes of music literature and 2,677 scores.

MANNHEIM, Städt Volks- und Musikbücherei est. 1914. 2,114 volumes of music literature. 6,607 scores, 1,577 records, 5 record players, 1 tape recorder and 2 listening studios. Arranges chamber music evenings and record concerts.

MULHEIM/RUHR, Städtbücherei- musikbücherei est. 1927. 1,503 volumes of music literature, 5,450 scores and 1 music room.

MUNICH, Städtische Musikbibliothek. 8,605 volumes of musical literature, 81,859 scores, 3,500 miniature scores, 1,200 full scores and 2,741 gramophone records. 57 periodicals are taken and the first volume of the catalogue was published in 1931, compiled by Willy Krienitz. The library was founded in 1902 and special collections include folk-songs, autographs and over 50,000 news cuttings. Has a piano, 1 record player, 2 tape recorders, 1 listening and recording studio, 4 music rooms, and arranges concerts of chamber music and works of Munich composers.

NEUMÜNSTER, Musikbücherei est. 1920. 850 volumes of music literature and 4,322 scores.

NEURENBURG, Städt Musikbücherei est. 1924. 2, 898 volumes of music literature and 9,894 scores.

PASSAU, Europe Bücherei d. Städt Passau/Musikapt est. 1955. 326 volumes of music literature, 2,000 scores, 301 records, 1 record player and 1 listening studio. Arranges record concerts.

REMSCHEID, Städt Bücherei/Musikbücherei est. 1952. 1,077 volumes of music literature, 2,798 scores, 68 records, 1 record player and 1 piano. Has music evenings.

TÜBINGEN, Stiftung Preussischer Kulturbesitz. Der Leiter des Tübinger Depots der ehen. Preuss. Staatsbibliothek. Special collections include:

Printed music dated before 1700.
240 volumes of music literature printed before 1700.
400 volumes from the Amalien- Bibliothek, consisting preponderantly of practical music of the 18th century, 300 mss including missals, choirbooks and tablatures.
40 volumes of autographs, especially of J. S. Bach and his family (90); Beethoven (50); J. Haydn (2); Mozart (70); and Schubert (15).

VIERSEN, Niederrheinische Volksliedarchiv. The essential material consists of 3,000 folk-songs of the Lower Rhine in the authentic form and 100 folk dances picked up from folk musicians. There are also symphonies performed by amateur music societies in the 18th and 19th centuries. A small collection of scores and 150 tapes.

WIESBADEN, Musikbücherei est. 1938. 5,168 volumes and scores, 285 records and 1 record player.

WUPPERTAL, Städt bibliotheque/Musikapt. 2,507 volumes of music literature, 8, 948 scores, 204 records, 1 record player and has record recitals.

GREECE

ATHENS, The Gennadius Library, American School of Classical Studies, Athens. The collections in the Gennadeion include Byzantine music with a complete set of *Monumenta Musicae Byzantine* which is in progress. There is the Greek liturgy and parts thereof, and works in modern Greek on church music in Greece today, including scores. There are also scores and texts of modern Greek folk music. In all, about 150 titles with a further 20 manuscripts of Byzantine religious music.

HOLLAND

AMSTERDAM, Openbare Muziekbibliotheek, Public Library, Eerste Jacob van Campenstraat 59, Amsterdam. 8,000 volumes of music literature; 37,000 scores and 1,900 records. The Toonkunst Bibliotheck has 10,000 volumes of early printed music, theoretical works, manuscripts, microfilms, autograph letters and modern scholarly editions. The arrangement of the material is according to instruments, voices and combinations, and not by genres such as sonatas, songs, motets, preludes and so on.

AMSTERDAM, Stichtung Donemus, 2,785 compositions bearing the Donemus copyright, divided into 738 orchestral, 350 vocal-orchestral, 1,014 chamber and 512 vocal-chamber music plus 171 a cappella chorus. There are 280 volumes of musical literature, 68 periodicals, 225 records and 2,575 tape recordings. The library controls the Alsbach collection of 14,800 compositions by 1,900 Dutch composers, published in Holland or abroad since the beginning of the 19th century. Besides being a library, Donemus is also the publisher of music scores and parts, a quarterly magazine *Sonorum Speculum*, and an audio-visual series of records and scores four times a year. Donemus published a *Catalogue of Vocal Music* in 1961 by composers affiliated to them; a *Catalogue of A Capella choir music in 1958*; and a *Catalogue of instrumental music* in 1959 by affiliated composers.

GRAVENHAGE, Gemeentemuseum's – Municipal Museum. P.O. Box. 72, The Hague. Has 20,000 volumes of music literature: 30,000 scores plus 7,500 full scores, and 250 records. Special collections include books and articles on ethno-musicology and on organology: a large collection of scores, vocal scores and libretti on the music of the theatre; the library of *Théâtre français de la Haye* from 1750–1875; 250 items of Lisztiana; about 50 archives of Dutch composers from 1875; several thousands of letters; prints and playbills, mostly Dutch. This is principally a research library with unusual literature and music before 1800. An illustrated printed brochure has recently been issued on musical instruments of the world

in their collections, titled *Gids buiten – europese muziekinstrumenten.*
1962.

HAARLEM, Stadsbibliotheek. 3,000 volumes of music literature;
11,000 scores; 1,200 miniature and 150 full scores. Special emphasis
is placed on organ literature as the town contains several old organs
and it has been the centre for organists who have come from all
over the world to the Summer School. Since 1951, an International
Improvisation concours has been held.

THE HAGUE, Openbare Musickbibliotheek. 3,000 volumes of
music literature, 32,000 scores, 5,000 miniature scores, 1,500 full
scores and 600 gramophone records.

UTRECHT, Instituut voor Muziekwetenschap der Rijksuniversiteit. 30,000 volumes of music literature; 15,000 scores; 2,000
gramophone records and 61 periodicals. Two monographs have
already been issued, in 1958 and 1960, of a series *Utrechtse Bijdragen
tot de Muziekwetenschap.* Valuable liturgical mss are held of the
12th–15th centuries. The University Institute of Musicology has a
large general library of its own whilst the Collegium Musicum has
orchestral parts and other musical items which are valuable source
materials for the study of 18th-century music in Holland.

The Institute has the disposal of a duplicate of the famous
Photogramm-Archiv of the National-Bibliothek of Vienna. In
addition, there is a complete collection of photostats and microfilms
of the works of Josquin Desprez and Jacob Obtrecht, and a music
incipit catalogue of works by composers of the Netherlands Schools of
the 15th and 16th centuries. Professor Dr Albert Smijers collected
this material in the first place and prepared the catalogue. Dr Myro-
slav Autonowycz continues the researches.

ITALY

FLORENCE, Biblioteca Marucelliana. Although not a library
specializing in music, it holds musical works and an important
collection of operatic libretti. There are no catalogues of works
acquired prior to 1925, but since then, 12,993 volumes and operas
have been obtained. Some printed works of the 16th century are
held.

MILAN, Biblioteca Nazionale Braidense. Has no special department of music but has liturgical mss, incunabula, and printed books

of the 16th–19th centuries; many old printed books on musical theory and literature, especially of the 18th century; a rich collection of opera libretti and some printed music of the 16th–18th centuries. More information on this latter collection of music can be found in *Fontes artes musicae 1960–62*, by Mariangela Donä under the article headed *Musiche a stampa nella Biblioteca Braidense di Milano*.

The liturgical library of the Duchy of Parma is not especially musical and only a few liturgical books contain music notation.

MODENA, Bibliotheca Estense. 3,837 items including mss of the 15th century, with Dunstable and his contemporaries well represented. There are many 18th-century operas and oratorios, including works by Mozart and mss by Stradella and Scarlatti. Printed works are almost all Italian and French of the 16th, 17th and 18th centuries. An important collection.

ROME, Biblioteca Nazionale Centrale Vittorio Emanuele II. Does not have a separate stock of music. Scores are sent to the Library of the St Cecilia Musical Academy. There is some liturgical music of the 15th–17th centuries and a few manuscripts of the 16th–17th centuries including works by Palestrina, Animuccia, Anerio, Santini, Vulpio and Scarlatti.

ROME, Casanatense. This is not a library specializing in music but it has 744 printed works and 113 manuscripts, the result of the Fondo Baini bequest. Baini was the biographer of Palestrina. In addition, there are a further 275 manuscripts mostly of the 18th century, including Scarlatti.

MALAYA

SINGAPORE, National Library. 380 volumes of music literature, 2,951 scores, 688 miniature scores and 142 full scores. In addition, there are 140 volumes of orchestral music available for loan to recognized musical societies, which include Chamber works, Vocal Scores, Opera, Oratorios, Cantatas and Musical plays.

NEW ZEALAND

AUCKLAND, Public Libraries, 4,112 volumes of music literature, 12,365 scores, 589 miniature scores, 378 full scores, and 2,415 records. In addition there is a collection of 827 volumes of vocal and instrumental music, plus literature on the technique of singing, the teaching and organization of music classes in schools and the history of music. The collection is financed by profits from the Auckland Secondary Schools' Music festival and a subsidy from the Auckland City Council. Items are available to both library users and schools alike.

A choral collection of over 200 works is drawn upon by choirs from all over New Zealand who pay a small hiring fee of 1d per copy per month plus postage both ways. The Harold Baxter collection comprises about 375 works with parts for small orchestra. A vertical file of musical clippings, concerning New Zealand in general and Auckland in particular, is being extended.

AUCKLAND, University Library. 1,500 volumes of music literature, 2,700 scores, 1,600 full and miniature scores, and 450 gramophone records.

WELLINGTON, Public Library. 1,852 volumes of music literature, 3,983 scores, 426 miniature scores, 3,557 full scores, 5,861 gramophone records including 3,261 at 78 r.p.m. which can only be played on the premises. There are two record-playing rooms, one for 78s and one for L.P.s. The latter are borrowed on a rental basis of 2s 6d per record and 2s for each additional disc, and cover the classics, plays, poetry, prose works and recordings of folk music.

NORWAY

BERGEN off Bibliothek, Strømgatan 6. Bergen. Has 3,400 volumes of music literature; 32,650 scores plus 670 miniature and 23 full scores; and 986 records. In 1906 Edward Grieg donated all his letters, 3,500 of them, his manuscripts (108 originals) and other items to the library. Two different catalogues of the collection have been issued, the latest an elegant production titled *Katalog over Griegutstillingen*, a list of the mss, first editions, letters and Griegiana exhibited in May and June 1962. In April 1962 the library obtained the unique collection of the first editions of Grieg's works from the Danish antiquarian, Dan Fog.

OSLO, Deichmanske Bibliotek. 2,211 volumes of musical literature and 5,004 scores. Monthly concerts are given during the autumn and winter seasons.

OSLO, Norsk Musikksamling, Universitets biblioteket. 14,000 volumes of music literature; 91,500 scores; 2,000 miniature and 1,000 full scores, plus 700 records. The collection was established in 1927 and it is the national depository for Norwegian-printed music. Mss number 7,000 comprising some 10,000 Norwegian folk-tunes, and all posthumous works of several Norwegian composers, including Fartein Valen, Ole Olsen, Johan Backer Lunde, Agathe og Fridtjof, Backer Grøndahl. A testamentary gift included almost all the literature of Beethoven and the library has copies of all preserved mss of Schubert's songs.

POLAND

KRAKOW, Biblioteka Jagiellónska. 4,000 volumes of music litera-ture, 30,000 scores. 220 periodicals and 900 gramophone records. Has 1,000 mss. Publications include: J. Reiss *Catalogue of music in the Biblioteka Jagiellónska of the 15th–18th centuries*, in three parts pub-lished between 1924 and 1938: W. Hordynski *Dziat nut w Biblioteka Jagiellónska*. Krakow, 1935 *in Przeglad Biblioteczny*, part 9, 1935.

WROCLAW (formerly BRESLAU) University Library. 17,100 volumes of music literature and 760 scores. The library enjoys the compulsory deposit of all music printed in Poland and it has some rare editions of early music. For example, *Zielenski Mikolaj: Com-muniones and Offertoria totius anni. Ven. 1611*. There are missals and antiphoners amongst the early mss. During the World War 1939–45, the collections of early music from the former town and University Libraries were partly destroyed. An up-to-date catalogue of the existing collection will contain about 1,200 titles plus 3,600 part-books. The collection transferred from the Brieg Gymnasium is still intact and details of it can be found in Friedrich Kuhn's *Beschrei-bendes Verzeichnis der Alten Musikalien*: *Handschriften und Drückwerke des Königlichen Gymnasium zu Brieg*. Leipzig 1897. There is a printed catalogue of early music: Emil Bohn *Bibliographie der Musik-Drück-werke bis 1700*. Berlin 1883.

The greater part of the collection of the Akademisches Institut für Kirchenmusik, the chapter library, is now in the Music Depart-ment of the University Library of Warsaw.

SOUTH AFRICA

CAPE TOWN, South Africa Public Library. 1,576 volumes of

music literature, 123 scores and miniature scores and 59 records. 28 periodicals are taken. In 1953, the John Armstrong collection of vocal music was presented by Mrs Armstrong in memory of her husband. Works other than those in ms may be borrowed by Inter-Library loan. There are printed and card catalogues of these 860 items which include solo songs, folk-songs, Minnesänge, vocal excerpts, songs by individual composers, part songs, choral works, sacred songs, anthems, liturgies, psalms, masses, carols, oratorios, cantatas, operas, masques, chamber and orchestral music.

CAPE TOWN, University Music Library. 5,000 volumes of music literature, 19,000 scores, 2,100 miniature scores, 1,005 full scores and 6,700 gramophone records. A catalogue of music manuscripts of William Henry Bell (1873–1946) was compiled by L. E. Taylor in 1948. Professor Bell was the first Professor at U.C.T., first Dean of the Faculty of Music and founder of the University's Little Theatre in 1930, where many of his dramatic musical compositions were first performed. The music department was formed in 1943 from the amalgamation of the collection of printed music, books on music and gramophone records then in the College of Music, and the music section and parts of the dramatic art section of the Jagger Library, the headquarters of the University of Cape Town Library system.

The Library is the first completely self-contained, functionally designed Music Library in South Africa. In 1958, the collection of the South African branch of the International Society of Contemporary Music was presented to the University, consisting of 800 scores.

Special collections include:

(a) Van Hulsteyn Collection of chamber music donated by Sir William van Hulsteyn.

(b) A School music collection, commenced in 1961, of scores, books, and gramophone records to assist students of music.

(c) Rare editions, including a facsimile copy of the original manuscript of Verdi's *Falstaff* published by La Scala, Milan in 1952 on the occasion of the 50th anniversary of Verdi's death, and a photolithographic edition of Beethoven's complete works.

(d) A collection of South African music comprising gramophone records of African music recorded by the African Music

Society; original manuscripts of South African composers and printed music with South African Associations.

JOHANNESBURG, Public Library. 3,988 volumes of music literature, 24,205 scores, 2,760 miniature scores and 2,199 full scores and orchestral sets which are sent to all parts of South Africa, Rhodesia and South-west Africa. A picture collection of opera productions, instruments, symphony orchestras and artists of all nationalities is being extended. Indexes of song titles and pianoforte works contained in anthologies are maintained. Lunch-time record recitals are given by the library staff twice weekly and it is hoped to establish a gramophone record lending collection shortly.

SPAIN

BARCELONA, Bibliotec Central. 5,369 volumes of music literature, 12,230 scores, 10,521 miniature scores and 1,709 full scores. The Department of Music has published 19 books on the organ, on instruments and on Spanish vocal music of the 13th–18th centuries. A catalogue of the library *Diputatio de Barcelona* was published in 1908–9 in 2 volumes. Special collections include opera libretti of the 18th and 19th centuries: musical iconographies; autographed scores and correspondence of the composers Felipe Pedrell and Isaac Albeniz. A specialized library for the study of Wagner and his works was provided by the illustrious Wagnerian Joaquin Pena. There are musical and photographic archives of codices existing in Spanish cathedrals and monasteries.

SWEDEN

ESKILSTUNA Stadsbibliotek. 975 volumes of music literature; 2,040 scores; 207 miniature scores and 860 gramophone records. A small music library operating from a manor house of just over 100 years old. A duplicated catalogue has been issued of the gramophone records.

GENTOFTE KOMMUNEBIBLIOTEK. 1,074 volumes of music literature; 5,572 scores; 560 miniature scores and 93 full scores. Uses the Universal Decimal Classification.

HOLMSTAD Stadsbibliotek. 494 volumes of music literature, 519 scores, 79 miniature scores and 392 gramophone records.

HUSKVARNA Stadsbibliotek. 222 volumes of music literature; 325 scores and 235 gramophone records.

KARLSKRONA, Stadsbiblioteket. 230 volumes of music literature, 141 scores, 94 miniature scores and 265 gramophone records in a collection established in July 1962.

KRISTIANSANDS Stadsbibliotek. 447 volumes of music literature; 126 scores; 40 miniature scores and 572 gramophone records.

LANDSKRONA Stadsbibliotek. 332 volumes of music literature, 270 scores and 360 gramophone records.

LULEA Stadsbibliotek. 700 volumes of music literature; 220 score and 1,000 gramophone records.

MALMBERGET, Gällivare – Malmbergets Folkbibliotek. 260 scores and 550 gramophone records.

MALMO, Stadsbibliotek. One of the most compact and luxurious music libraries I have seen. It occupied new premises soon after the War. Opened in 1958, beautifully furnished and generously provided for, this special music department houses 2,000 books, 3,300 music scores, home and foreign periodicals, and over 1,000 records. These are of classical music, of language and speech. As far as equipment goes, there are 3 H.M.V. gramophones, 3 amplifiers, 12 earphones on tables in the room, a loud speaker and a Grundig radio. There are two listening cubicles as the records are meant for hearing in the library, and are only lent to lecturers and study circles. The staff consists of two professional librarians and the department is open 43 hours a week, including 4 hours on Sundays for 6 months of the year. The fittings and equipment cost 18,000 Swedish crowns (£1,300 approx.) and they were given by the Friends of the Library group.

NACKA Stadsbibliotek. 167 volumes of music literature; 990 scores; 26 miniature scores; and 305 gramophone records.

NORRKÖPING City Library. 835 volumes of music literature, 2,585 scores, 325 miniature scores, 20 periodicals and 350 gramophone records.

ÖMSKÖLDSVIKS, Stadsbibliotek. 200 volumes of music literature, 40 miniature scores and 160 gramophone records.

ÖREBRO, Stadsbibliotek. 600 volumes of music literature; 2,900 scores and 300 gramophone records.

SOLNA, Stadsbibliotek. 622 volumes of music literature, 403 scores and 1,368 records. A stencilled catalogue of the record collection has been issued and has annual supplements. A new library building is to be opened in 1964 which will house a special music department.

STOCKHOLM, Kungliga biblioteket. (The Royal Library), Box 5039, Stockholm 5. The collection consists chiefly of Swedish music, the main collection of foreign music in print and manuscript being housed in the Library of the Academy of Music. It contains about 50,000 volumes, the books including all those printed in Sweden. For the holdings of foreign music see Åke Davidsson, *Catalogue* . . . *des Imprimés de Musique des XVIe et XVIIe Siècles conservés dans les Bibliothèques Suédoises*, Upsala 1952 and C. G. Stellan Mörner, *Rariteter ur en okatalogiserad notsamling i Kungl. biblioteket i Stockholm* (in Studier tillägnade. Carl Allan Moberg. Svensk tidskrift för musikforskning 1961).

Among mss (autographs) : works by Roman, Hurlebusch, Berwald and K. B. Blomdahl ('Aniara'). A collection of letters written by Jenny Lind.

Since 1960 there is a National Record Archive in existence at the library, of which the main task is to collect all commercial sound material relating to Sweden. In July 1962 this archive contained about 7,000 records and 100 tapes.

See : A. Esdaile, *National Libraries of the World*, second ed., London 1957, pp. 224–232.

STOCKHOLM, Kungl. Musikaliska Akademieus Bibliotek. 40,000 volumes of music literature; 600,000 scores; 150 periodicals and 1,000 gramophone records in the Royal Conservatory of Music for teaching purposes. Has published :

(a) Åke Lellky, *Katalog over orkester − och Körverk.*

(b) Cari Johannson, *French music publishers catalogues of the second half of the 18th century.*

Special collections and features :

(a) F. Hallardt's collection (to the library in 1795), very comprehensive, containing music from the 18th century in mss and first-editions especially by Mannheimer School – and Italian composers.

(*b*) A similar collection of considerable value is the Patrick Alströmer collection (1949).

(*c*) Johan Mazer's collection (1847) contains about 3,000 works, mss and first-editions, especially chamber music from the 18th and the first decades of the 19th centuries, symphonies and vocal music, the whole collection very costly bound in full leather bindings with gold ornamentations.

(*d*) The great collection in the Royal Swedish Opera of 18th-century opera scores and orchestral parts is now deposited in this library.

(*e*) P. A. Fouché d'Otrante's collection (1858) and Gustaf G. G. Oxenstierna collection (1860) both contain operas (mss and first-editions) from the 17th and 18th centuries, in full scores and vocal scores mostly by Italian and French composers.

These six collections make this library one of the most important in Europe concerning 18th-century music.

(*f*) The collection of the German Church in Stockholm (1874) contains vocal music from the 16th and 17th centuries, i.e. Schein Diletti pastorali and Eucharius Hoffmann, 24 Cantiones; Orlando di Lasso, Palestrina, Schultz, and others.

(*g*) C. O. Boije's af Gennäs collection (1924) guitar music. Among other collections of interest are Adelina Patti's and Christine Nilsson's, both containing vocal scores of operas.

Among mss (autographs): J. Haydn, Symphony No. 49 (*La Passione*); M. Haydn, Three Masses; Mozart, Sketch of a scene of Titus; Beethoven, Sketch of a movement for string quartet Op. 95 and a sketch of a piano sonata; G. Albrechtsberger, G. Charpentier, P. Dukas, E. Du Puy, J. L. Dussek, E. Grieg, Gaveau, F. Liszt, J. B. Lully, I. Moscheles, C. Nielsen, F. Pedrell, B. Romberg, G. Rossini, Clara Schumann, J. Sibelius, P. Tjajkovskij, C. M. v. Weber; also a great collection of Swedish autographs, I. A. Franz Berwald, W. Peterson-Berger, J. H. Roman, E. S. Sjögren, W. Stenhammar, Aug. Söderman.

Items are lent to students and to other libraries. The vast collection of orchestral scores and parts is lent to Swedish orchestral societies.

STOCKHOLM, Stadsbibliotek. 1,670 volumes of music literature,

720 scores, 119 miniature scores and 232 records. An excellent printed catalogue of books on the fine arts, music and the theatre, acquired up to 1945, was published in 1949, entitled *Katalog över Skön Konst, musik och teater.*

VASTERÅS, Stifts-och landesbiblioteket. This must be one of the finest libraries, architecturally, for the size of the town, in the world. There are 1,186 volumes of music literature; 462 scores; 183 miniature scores and 1,243 gramophone records. An excellent catalogue of the record collection, stencilled but with an attractive laminated cover, was issued in 1962. It comprises all records acquired up to the end of 1961 and will be supplemented at intervals. Vasterås has a Chapter and College Library of incunabula and manuscripts, and here are vocal and orchestral parts formerly belonging to the High School, and acquired prior to 1850. A catalogue of them was issued in 1917.

U.S.A.

AUSTIN, TEXAS. University Music Library. 10,000 volumes of music literature; 7,500 scores; 3,000 miniature scores and 2,800 gramophone records. A monthly acquisition list of records is published. A general collection of generous proportions with numerous collected editions.

BOSTON, NEW ENGLAND. Conservatory of Music. 8,132 volumes of music literature, 14,802 scores, 488 miniature scores, 1,474 full scores, 5,600 gramophone records and 58 periodicals. Special collections include the Geraldine Farrar collection of her own opera scores; the Preston collection of mss by 55 famous musicians; and a collection of ancient instruments with especial emphasis on the oriental.

BUFFALO AND ERIE County Public Library: Grosvenor Music Division. 53,000 volumes of music literature and scores, and 27,700 records. 50 periodicals are taken. There are many works in ms and facsimile and an extensive collection of historical editions and complete editions of the great composers. The collection of Americana includes many first editions, early and rare songsters, and 69,000 song sheets. On July 1, 1954 the Grosvenor Library merged with the Buffalo Public Library and the Erie County Public Library, and became the Grosvenor Music Division.

CHICAGO, Public Library. 9,300 volumes of music literature, 28,800 scores, 3,000 miniature scores, 75 full scores, 110 periodicals, 900 bound volumes of back numbers of music periodicals and 13,000 records. There are 2,500 old popular songs dating from 1830 for reference and historical purposes: 5,000 records for earphone listening on the premises, and a growing collection of full operatic scores. Record concerts are held weekly and live concerts featuring local talent from October to the National Music Week in May. Printed publications cover the Music Department: the Symphony, the Song and the Opera in books, on records and in scores; and Non-Musical Recordings.

DETROIT Public Library, Music and Performing Arts Department. 12,000 volumes of music literature; 65,635 scores; 1,434 miniature and full scores; 125 periodicals and 20,000 gramophone records. In addition, has 7,000 items of popular sheet music of historical interest, analytically indexed, with a song index on cards and 45,332 choral parts. Special collections include: (a) the Michigan collection of works by Michigan composers and writers; (b) the Azalia Hackley Memorial Collection which attempts to record the achievements of negroes in all the performing arts, through books, scores, recordings, programmes, photographs, newspaper and magazine cuttings.

The library has the only separate performing arts department in an American public library and its staff of 11 includes performers who engage actively in the musical life of the city. This large collection is aimed at the scholar and practical musician, and there are complete holdings of microcards from the University of Rochester, Sibley Music Library, to compensate for the lack of rarities.

EVANSTON, ILLINOIS. North-western University Music Library. 16,200 volumes of music literature, 13,150 scores and 8,050 gramophone records. There are 158 reels of microfilm representing 813 volumes and 450 titles of music books and periodicals on microcards. The library was organized on a full-time basis as recently as 1945 and tremendous growth has taken place since then.

PITTSBURGH, Carnegie Library. 20,000 volumes of music literature, 40,000 scores and 8,050 records. This is a reference and lending library with emphasis for lending purposes on editions of music since 1700 in all media of performance. The reference collection includes early and first editions, collected works of major composers, monumental sets and historical anthologies, bibliographies, thematic catalogues and other standard English and foreign reference books. The 230 periodicals filed commence in the year 1798 and include a notable collection of 19th-century American music journals.

PROVIDENCE Public Library, Kentucky. 3,500 volumes of music literature: 16,794 scores and 300 miniature scores; 6,000 gramophone records. Special collections include works by Rhode Island composers, including some manuscripts: Civil War music, especially broadside ballads and early New England Music.

ROCHESTER, NEW YORK. Sibley Music Library, the University of Rochester. Eastman School of Music. Founded in 1904 by Hiram W. Sibley. There being no city library at the time, the nucleus of the collection was deposited in the University Library. Upon the founding of the Eastman School of Music, the Sibley Music Library was moved into the Student and Faculty Lounge in the main building of the school. Its duties were to serve the curriculum of the school as well as providing a music library for the citizens of Rochester. In 1938, the library moved into a new building altogether.

The Pougin collection on theatre and opera in France during the 17th and 18th centuries was acquired in 1923. The 11th-century 'Reichenan Codex', one of the earliest complete mss in America on the subject of music, was purchased in 1929 from the private library of Dr Werner Wolffheim in Berlin. Seven years later, it acquired the 12th-century 'Admont-Rochester Codex 494', a valuable treatise on the musical scholarship of the Middle Ages. Other incunabula containing works by Finck, Gaffurio, Keinspeck and Niger, and mss of early musical notation from the library of Oskar Fleischer are held. Autograph scores include Purcell, Mozart, Beethoven, Mendelssohn, Schumann, Liszt, Rubinstein, Brahms, Debussy, Fauré and Krenek, and the American composers Chadwick, Foote, Hill, Macdowell, Mason, Porter, Rogers, Thompson, Hanson, White, Harris, Copland, Bacon, Jutheil and Diamond, many of which are holograph scores. Autograph letters include Gluck, Handel, Franz and Berlioz.

The Renaissance and Baroque periods are represented by the Olschki Collection of sacred music, some unique copies of 16th-century Italian madrigal books, the Petrucci printing of the Masses of Josquin Desprez, the 1546–1551 part books of the Masses of

Cristobal Morales, and the complete *Magnum Opus musicum* of Orlando di Lasso.

Other collections include the viola music from the library of Samuel Belov; over 2,000 compositions from the string music library of Jacques Gordon; 964 operas of the 1880–1930 period; the violin library of Ben Dennof; facsimile editions of contemporary American music, and 2,000 records from Record Hunter.

The University of Rochester Press has published reproductions in micro-card form of valuable theoretical and historical works. These are listed in a catalogue *Microcard Publications in Music* published by the Press in July 1960.

The Sibley Library now contains 120,000 volumes of books and music, 25,000 uncatalogued songs, sheet music and pamphlets, microfilms and microcards, and is reputed to be one of the best equipped music research libraries on the American continent.

st louis Public Library. 21,094 scores, 75 periodicals and 14,583 gramophone records. Has collected editions of Bach, Beethoven, Brahms, Chopin, Corelli, Dvořák, Mozart and Vivaldi. Also Denk-mäler der Tonkunst in Osterreich, and the Foster Hall reproductions of Stephen Collins-Foster's songs and compositions.

washington, University Music Library. 5,000 volumes of music literature, 15,000 scores. 90 periodicals, 13,500 gramophone records and 1,500 tapes. Special collections include the American Music Centre of 1,000 items of and about American music, including tune books, Lowell Mason materials, and early popular ballads.

Subject Index

to the Classification Tables
on pages 55 to 61

Index to Text

172   INDEX

Tottenham Public Libraries, 98
Transcribers: cataloguing, 81
Trinity College, London, 19, 20
Trinity College, Cambridge, 120
Trinity College, Dublin, 121
Tübingen Stiftung Preussischer Kulturbesitz, 142
Tunbridge Wells Public Libraries, 98
Tunks, Dorothy E., 7
Turnbull, Robert, 88
Twickenham Public Libraries, 98

United Music Publishers *Ltd*, 42
University of London, 128
Utrecht. Institutet voor Muziekwetenschap der Rijksuniversiteit, 144

Vasterås Stifts-och landesbiblioteket, 153
Vaughan Williams Trust, 99
Versailles. Bibliothèque municipale classée, 135
Victoria and Albert Museum, 128
Victoria, *Queen*, 19
Viersen Niederrheinische Volksliedarchiv, 142
Voltaire, François Marie Arouet, 18
Vox, 27

Wakefield Public Libraries, 98
Wales. National Library, 117
Walford Davies, *Sir* Henry. *See* Davies, *Sir* Henry Walford
Wallasey Public Libraries, 98
Walpole, *Sir* Robert, 18
Walsall Public Libraries, 98
Walthamstow Public Libraries, 36, 98
Wandsworth Public Libraries, 98
Warrington Public Libraries, 98
Warwickshire County Libraries, 98
Washington University Music Library, 156

Watford Public Libraries, 98
Watson, Henry: Music Library, Manchester, 38
Weekes, A. *and* Co. *Ltd*, 39
Wellington Public Library, 146
Welsh National Opera Company, 23
Wesley, John, 18
West Ham Public Libraries, 98
West Riding County Libraries, 99
West Suffolk County Libraries, 99
West Sussex County Libraries, 99
Western Australia. Library Board, 131
Westminster Central Music Library, 99
Westmorland Public Libraries, 91
Widnes Public Libraries, 100
Wiesbaden Musikbücherei, 142
Wigan Public Libraries, 100
Wighton collection, 87
Willesden Public Libraries, 100
Wilson, B. *and* L. *Ltd*, 41
Wiltshire County Libraries, 100
Wireless Trade News, 30
Wolverhampton Public Libraries, 100
Wood, Charles, 118
Wood, *Sir* Henry J., 14
—— : collection, 127
Woolwich Public Libraries, 100
Worcester Cathedral Library, 130
Worcestershire County Libraries, 100
Workington Public Libraries, 100
Worthing Public Libraries, 100
Wroclaw University Library, 147
Wuppertal Stadt bibliotheque/ Musikapt, 142

York Minster Library, 130
York Public Libraries, 100

Zavertal, Ladislas Joseph Philip Paul, 100
Zavertal collection, 128

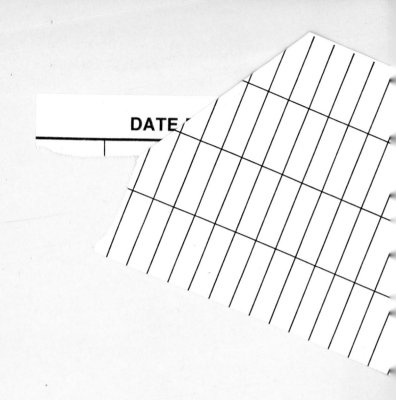

DATE